More True Tales From a Cemetery Cop

Jaimie Vernon

© 2016 Jaimie Vernon
Bullseye Canada Publishing
Toronto, Ontario, Canada

All rights reserved.
Unauthorized duplication is strictly prohibited.
The name Cemetery Cop, the motto "to serve and protect the dead" and the badge logo are trademarks of Bullseye.

Photographs and cover art by Jaimie Vernon

ISBN-13: 978-1540780584

OTHER BOOKS/E-BOOKS
by
Jaimie Vernon

Life's A Canadian Blog: Pop Culture Essays From North of the 49th Parallel (2012)

Life's A Canadian Punk: Who Wants Guns? The Swindled Story 1973-1983 (2013)

The Canadian Pop Music Encyclopedia: Volume 1 - A thru K (2012)

The Canadian Pop Music Encyclopedia: Volume 2 – L thru Z (2013)

True Tales From a Cemetery Cop (2016)

E-BOOKS
by
Jaimie Vernon

Life's A Canadian Blog 2: How To Succeed In the Music Business with Zero Talent (2014)

THE TIME LAPSE HUMANITIES BOOK 0
A Sci-Fi series
Chrestomathy 1: Miss Arlington Springs 11, 473 B.P.
Chrestomathy 2: Point of Conception

JAIMIE VERNON

CONTENTS

Acknowledgments	i
Introduction	3
Chapter One	8
Chapter Two	20
Chapter Three	40
Chapter Four	52
Chapter Five	67
Chapter Six	84
Chapter Seven	97
Chapter Eight	110
Chapter Nine	120
Chapter Ten	129
Chapter Eleven	141
About the Author	147

ACKNOWLEDGMENTS

To Sharon, Riley and Danielle who stuck by me despite enduring a year without me as I worked shifts beyond exhaustion and tried my best to be 'normal' when I got home. I know you sacrificed a lot. Love you.

To the security crew and cemetery staff for offering up some of their own experiences for this book.

To Barb DiGiulio, Ben Harrison, and Mark Tang whose 'Nightside' radio show allowed me to talk about the Cemetery Cop to a wider audience.

To Bob Reid, Karen Borgal, Michael Tomasek, and Gail Dusome for the critical eye in editing.

To all those who supported *'True Tales From a Cemetery Cop'*. I couldn't have done a second one without you.

To Janice Richardson for the advice and the cover quote!

INTRODUCTION

In September of 2016 I decided to write down my recollections of working as a security guard in a cemetery. It was actually five cemeteries, but for the sake of the narrative and to keep the confidentiality of the people involved, I created an amalgam of those cemeteries, and gave it the fictional name of Beacon Hill. It was there that I could set the tone and the visceral arena for all the unbelievable things that happened to me over a period of one-year starting in September 2014 and ending in September 2015.

For such a seemingly harmless place where people are laid to rest the graveyard was filled with everything necessary to create good drama, pathos, and comedy. I went with my gut and I wrote through my mind's eye in recreating the sights, sounds, and conversations from many harrowing and increasingly normalized encounters. After all, the mandate of the security company that I worked for was "observe and report," and it became the lens through which I would populate the world of Beacon Hill Cemetery.

I released the book *True Tales From a Cemetery Cop* on October 3, 2016, and the positive reaction to it was immediate. Social media, which can be a fickle mistress at the best of times, ran with it. Those who have known me a long time read it. Those who followed my exploits in the music business – and specifically through my online through Bob Segarini's *'Don't Believe a Word I Say'* blog - read it.

I became a member of an online forum called Goodreads that is another social media platform for people that like to read and the authors whose words they enjoy. Reviews came in from strangers. I made the acquaintance of Janis Richardson who is a retired funeral director and has written her own twist on her cemetery experiences called *Winter's Mourning (A Spencer Funeral Home Niagara Cozy Mystery)*.

What I thought was a dark and limited subject matter designed as psychotherapy for myself seems to have a mass appeal. Everyone can identify with the death of a loved one. The fact that I was out there defending the graves of those loved ones from predators and perverts made Cemetery Cop – the idealized version of me – someone to cheer for.

I've been on radio to talk about it already. Barb

True Tales From A Cemetery Cop

DiGiulio from *The Nightside* on NewsTalk1010 was an awesome host in bringing this odd vocation to light. The idea of turning the book into a movie or a TV show has also been thrown into conversations by many people. They believe that actor Kevin James should grab the rights to the book as the concept for *Paul Blart: Mall Cop Part 3*. I'm not against the idea, it's just that I find it all very flattering and surreal.

Like the security job itself, writing the first book was not a career decision but a necessity. I wanted it on record and out of my head because elements of that job still haunt me; for anyone that's read the book you'll know exactly what I'm talking about. Despite its modest print run and under-stated promotion, it continues to sell. It has been an exciting surprise. I don't get surprised much.

I've spent the better part of 40 years creating and selling *music*. I have never had any of my work accepted at this type of mainstream level before. I have decided that maybe I should take a little detour and see where this writing thing goes.

I had not planned to write a second book. In fact, I had planned to write two prequels: *True Tales From a Car Jockey* and *True Tales From a Civil Servant*. That's not to say I've abandoned either idea. Those will most definitely be pursued in the future. I've also got a few other writing projects piling up, but they are about music, and have no expiry date, so I can get to those later.

However, a second book of graveyard stories is a tall order. To me, *Cemetery Cop #1* had all my "A" material in it. These were the events that resonated the loudest with me, and I felt they were great human-interest stories. Those who read my early Facebook posts while I was originally on the job, and those who've since read the book, tend to agree. So, is there anything left in the reservoir of my old incident reports to satisfy a quality sequel? I believe there is.

Many stories were left out initially because of confidentiality issues that would have revealed the location of the cemetery and the people involved. I did not want to break their trust. It was a conundrum I didn't care to tackle at the time. After some legal advice, and the wise words of other authors in the same predicament, I've decided to revisit those stories and rework them in my own fictionalized way.

Recently I returned to my old haunts and discussed these issues with the many employees I interacted with including two security guards that trained me. They've given me consent to add them to the case files here. One guard you know as Billy from the first book. He returns in this book as the star of several more humorous and hair-raising stories.

I hope these tales act as an overview of what *all* Cemetery Cops go through. They are not unique to me. As empathetic humans, the themes of death and grief are universal. Read on as the Beacon Hill Cemetery story and its humble security guard continues…

The names contained herein have been changed to protect the privacy of the living. The cemetery referred to is a composite of the many places I had to patrol during my duties as a security guard and shall remain anonymous to protect the privacy of the dead, and the confidentiality of my former employer, the cemeteries and their staff respectively. All opinions are mine and not those of the security industry or the funeral industry.

True Tales From A Cemetery Cop

*** WARNING: THIS BOOK CONTAINS GRAPHIC DESCRIPTIONS OF FUNERALS, DEATH AND HUMAN REMAINS, ADULT SITUATIONS, AND COARSE LANGUAGE ***

Jaimie Vernon
November 2016

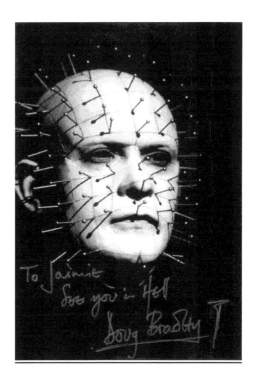

CHAPTER ONE

GROWING UP IN FEAR

It's apology time. It seems to me that my lack of fear of cemeteries was never convincingly explained in *True Tales From a Cemetery Cop*. I declared my immunity to such fears, and I was presumptuous in thinking the reader should just take it as fact. I dove into the job, and my stories, without much more than a casual "I don't get spooked." Thank you for playing along, but I feel I owe you more than a dismissive "don't be silly, I was a superhero in the graveyard" wave of the pen. I really am a more complicated person than that.

Bravery in the face of the unknown isn't necessarily a birth trait. I firmly believe we are the products of our environments. I've seen brothers and sisters grow up in the same households and become totally different and uniquely defined human beings based on their individual treatment in the home and what they then experienced outside of it. First born, middle child, last born, broken home, social inequity, financial burden and a host of other factors can be the difference between a well-adjusted and a deeply flawed human being. I can say with all honesty that I'm a flawed human being. It used to be a deep flaw, now it's just scar tissue. Working as a security guard at a cemetery actually helped heel some of those flaws. It wasn't always so.

I was born with blood clots in my head. Poor delivery technique? Forceps? Birth defect? No one knows. It was 1963 and Moms-to-be weren't given as much as an ultrasound to prepare them for what to expect. My doctor was Crawford Anglin – one of the heads of paediatrics at Sick Children's Hospital in Toronto. He was the best at what he did. They would eventually name parts of three hospitals after him. He reminded me of Marcus Welby, though his nurse was the opposite of him – playing the real life embodiment of Nurse Ratchet. He passed at the age of 98 in June 2016, having saved the lives of thousands of children.

At six months old it became obvious to him that there was something wrong with me. I couldn't hold my head up yet. There are late bloomers, he knew, but he didn't want to take any chances. They did a myriad of tests on me and discovered the blood clots. By the middle of 1964 it was time to operate. Anglin handed me over to the chief of the recently opened neurosurgery department at Sick Kids named Dr. E. Bruce Hendrick. He was Ben Casey to Anglin's Marcus, and he'd been recruited by Anglin from a hospital in New York City.

The operation went off without a hitch, at least medically. It took a toll on my Mom and Dad, though. I was in the hospital for several months. Mom came to my bedside every day, but my Dad had to work, and was limited to a few minutes each day if he could make it there before the end of visiting hours. Neither parent could form an effective bond with me while I was bandaged and still unable to communicate with either of them. That distance, that isolation, would remain even after I was brought home. My parents would always live in fear that I'd be taken away. In the pre-Bubble Wrap era of the early 1960s everyone put on a happy face, and suffered emotionally alone.

I can't really speak for my parents, but I know it must have been hard trying to live normally while I spent most of my early years trying to play catch up with the other kids.

Would I be visually or mentally impaired? Would I learn to walk and talk properly? It was all a crapshoot. My Mom did the best she could with me while my Dad continued being the breadwinner. Thankfully, as time would show, I was fine physically and mentally. Emotionally, I would be a train wreck. I was lonely and insecure. I acted the most like the person I was closest to – my mother – who was a hard-as-nails and brash disciplinarian. She was filled with a lot of anger. I was afraid of her and cried at the drop of a dime. My father couldn't handle my crying episodes. It was endemic for the times. Crying boys were weak. My parents weren't horrible people. They reacted the only way they knew how. As a child you can't understand this. It was inevitable that therapy was going to be part of my future.

I became an over-achiever to please them both. I nailed school. I made the track team. I excelled at visual art. I was also my mother's son and was mouthy as hell. I thought I knew it all. I became the centre of attention and other kids were not impressed in the least. In short order, the beatings from other kids at school began. It was probably around Grade 4. The more they hurt me the more I mouthed back. It was an endless cycle. I was small as a kid. My parents feared I wouldn't grow much past 5' 5" like my Dad. In that reality I was physically incapable of defending myself. I learned how to run fast. I spent years running back and forth to school to avoid being beaten. I would only find safety in class or in my house.

I suffered terrible nightmares as a child, clearly as a manifestation of my personal issues. I once killed a large wasp in my bedroom window, and that night had a dream that it was chasing me, and trying to kill me. I ended up jumping out of bed, leaving the comfort of our apartment, and hiding down a flight of stairs believing the wasp was coming to get me. My folks didn't get it. My Dad yelled at me because I'd woken everyone up in the apartment.

My peer group was pretty supportive, however. We were a tightly knit bunch of nerds, but I spent most of my time drawing attention to myself and embarrassing them – mostly because I had a huge chip on my shoulder, and had no idea how to articulate my anger. So my social skills were an endless drone of comedic quips and sarcasm.

Bullies don't understand sarcasm, and the beatings

continued right up until the first year of high school. My parents finally caught on that things weren't good in my world after three guys at school nearly drown me in the school swimming pool during gym class, then took my clothes and dumped them in a toilet in the girls' change room. I was George McFly to a gang of Biff Tannens.

Fortunately, I didn't stay a victim long after that as I switched schools, grew five inches, and joined a punk band. I had become fearless and never took another hit again. I compartmentalized my anger, rarely acted out, and adopted a steely façade. I became a loud, passive-aggressive curmudgeon before my time. It would prove to be effective against the various impediments at the cemetery decades later when I became a Cemetery Cop.

INVASION OF THE POPCORN SNATCHERS

I told you that story to tell you *this* one.

Aside from my life-long obsession with pop music I am also a dyed-in-the-wool, closet cinephile. I'm a sucker for a historical drama or an action film or cleverly scripted comedy. These are my go-to choices on a lazy Sunday afternoon when the best that television can offer is mindless tripe like *Flip Your Spouse*, *Lose Weight or Die* or the sermon of some rat bag preacher who is pick-pocketing the elderly through the very television itself. But I digress.

My movie genres of choice have always been Sci-Fi and Horror. I have my parents to thank/blame for this. As an impressionable child I lived in an area of Toronto that put us 500 feet from the late-lamented Cedarbrae Cinemas in Scarborough, and within 20 minutes driving distance from no less than five drive-in movie theatres. Note to Millennials reading this: a "drive-in" was a giant parking lot with a six-storey movie screen where you'd park your car and watch first-run movies with 200 other hapless motorists, and their families, and friends. That was a whole lot of silver screens before the invention of the SuperMegaGoogleplexiums and the HDTV redux version.

It was on the rarest of occasions that we went to Cedarbrae Cinema because they tended to show more adult fare on the two screens inside. I do recall one occasion when I was 8 1/2 where myself and a close friend were dropped off there by my mother with cash for the tickets and candy to see Disney's re-launch of *Pinocchio*; "See it one last time before it's locked in Disney's vaults again FOREVER!"

Well played Mr. Disney. Well played. However, after we'd bought our tickets I brow-beat my good friend into going to see the brand new Steve McQueen race car movie *Le Mans* that was playing on the second screen in the same building. So we sneaked in with the adult crowd and got to see what I thought was going to be a better film.

Problem was, the running time of *Pinocchio* was 88 minutes, while *Le Mans* was much longer at 106 minutes. So, when my friend and I didn't show up at the front of the theatre at the designated time for our parents to pick us up, they came in looking for us. We were hauled out of the movie and had our asses kicked all the way home. I believe I was grounded until I was 13. I finally saw the ending to *Le Mans* on TV in 2015 – ironically, during a lunch break working as the Cemetery Cop. I eventually saw *Pinocchio*, as well, with my kids. I came to realize it was one of Disney's darker morality tales: a wooden kid with a dysfunctional, erectile proboscis who is turned into a donkey, and spends a good part of that sequence screaming in pain along with other misbehaving kids. I found the imagery disturbing, and I'm glad I didn't see it that day at Cedarbrae Cinema.

The more common movie experience for my family was the drive-in. It was a welcome respite for my Mom & Dad because they'd stick my sister and me in pyjamas in hopes we'd fall asleep during the second half of a double feature. The four of us would pile into Dad's aquamarine, 1967, Plymouth Valiant, and off we'd go to one of the five area drive-ins depending on what was playing where. Our choices were: The Scarboro (at Kennedy & Lawrence), The Parkway (at Sheppard & the Don Valley Parkway), The North-East (at Esna Park, north of Steeles), The Teepee (on Liverpool Road in Pickering, Ontario) or The Bay-Ridges that was directly across the street from what is now the Pickering Town Centre, and located where Pickering City Hall and Library now stands.

My Dad was emphatic about going early so we could get a good spot in front of the screen. You didn't want to have to park behind the concession stand because it was always poor visibility for viewing the film, and too much visibility for observing teenage sex in the back of someone's family sedan.

The memories are vivid. Dad hit the snack bar early – 50 oz. bladder buster drinks? Check. 40 lb. tub of popcorn? Check. French Fries? Hot Dogs? Red licorice? Check, check, and check.

My sister and I would hit the playground in our pyjamas, and being the older of the two of us, I'd be tormented and ridiculed for it. I didn't care. It meant making temporary acquaintances for 10 or 15 minutes while we discussed what the movies were going to be about and hope, amongst all hope, we'd get to see some kid puke up his dinner after twenty spins on the Tilt-a-Whirl. That was worth the price of my Dad's $5.00 Family Value admission alone.

As the sun set behind the corrugated fencing of the parking lot - except at The Teepee, which had the disadvantage of facing *into* the setting sun - we'd hunker down for twilight time. Inevitably, my sister and I spent the night fighting for blankets, and trying to see past Mom & Dad's heads from the backseat. Either my sister would pass out or we had to interrupt the proceedings by going back to the concession stand to go pee. Of course, we'd miss 15 minutes of the movie because the line-ups were always so long.

These adventures are indelibly stamped in my brain. They are some of my earliest memories of childhood. I know this because the films I remember seeing at the drive-in begin when I was around 5 or 6 years old just after my sister was born such as *Planet of the Apes*, *2001: A Space Odyssey*, *Butch Cassidy & the Sundance Kid*, and others. I seem to recall some older movies doing a second run as filler features as well like 1962's *Day of the Triffids* - a movie that terrified me, and has haunted me to this day.

As we got older, Mom & Dad's frequency to the movies increased, and allowed us to catch the continuing saga of the *Planet of the Apes*, Michael Crichton's *Andromeda Strain*, *Airport*, the original *Westworld* (and its long forgotten sequel *Futureworld*), *Logan's Run'*, the Irwin Allen disaster flicks like *Poseidon Adventure* (and its insipid Maureen McGovern theme song "Morning After"), *Towering Inferno*, *Earthquake* and *Rollercoaster*. Yes, filmmakers were blowing up the planet long before Roland Emmerich made his first student film.

A lot of these movies were a bit alarming to kids our age with their plane crashes, burning buildings, tidal waves, sinking ships, earthquakes, and biological warfare. Fortunately, I was reassured by adults that living in Toronto, Ontario, I was never going to experience any of this (well, except maybe a burning building). But, here's where the Fear Factor began to come into play.

I was subjected to a myriad of terrifying – for a child – horror movies that were particular favourites of my Mom's. She delighted in gruesome blood and gorefests. My Dad never commented on them so I'm not sure how he felt about any of it. Movies like *Theatre of Blood*, *Let's Scare Jessica to Death*, *Tales From the Crypt*, *Children Shouldn't Play With Dead Things*, *Now the Screaming Starts*, and Karen Black's legendary performance in *Trilogy of Terror*. These were my initiation into the horror genre.

In hindsight, I was also lucky to have seen many UK imported screenings of the Hammer Horror classics with my cousin at a gymnasium-sized theatre located at the Canadian Forces Base Borden in Angus, Ontario, where she lived. Our folks would drop us there around noon on a Saturday, and we'd sit, or rather, food fight, through double, triple, and occasionally, quadruple bills. We got to see some of Christopher Lee's and Peter Cushing's cheesiest period of ghouls and ghosts epics like *Night Creatures* (aka *Captain Clegg*), *The Two Faces of Dr. Jekyll*, and *Terror of the Tongs*. I was both repelled and attracted to these movies about otherworldly evil and demons.

Alas, I eventually became immune to the jump-scares as films, in and of themselves, have a beat and tempo that are always predictable if you've seen enough of them. I'd become critical of the predictability and, let's be honest, horrible special effects.

I became jaded by most of everything offered. For instance, when I was finally old enough to see *The Exorcist* on television years after its release, I wasn't just disappointed, I laughed my ass off. The film had gained such legendary reputation that it couldn't live up to the hype that I'd heard about. It was a colossal letdown.

The underlying issue for me was that I didn't believe in God. Without the indoctrination in the fear of Hell, I had no reference point for what I was seeing on the screen. Demonic possession? Really? I couldn't suspend my disbelief. All I saw was a kid with werewolf eyes puking green soup that sounded like the Cookie Monster.

It didn't mean I wasn't fascinated by the idea of Heaven and Hell. As an outsider looking in, I wanted to know more about what made Christians tick – at least in the matters of Holy Damnation. It informed so much of what the horror genre was about that I wanted to understand what I was supposed to be afraid of.

I started reading horror fiction like *The Omen* series of books, Mary Shelley's *Frankenstein*, Bram Stoker's *Dracula*, and other classics. All of these were fascinating for sure, but they were really just studies into the dark side of the human condition. The presumed horror was left up to the imagination which I didn't manifest much of. I was a visceral guy. Tactile and interactive. If I couldn't see it with my own eyes I didn't much believe in it. My scepticism is legendary.

I'm not much of a Stephen King fan either. His early horror played out more as outrageous fantasy, and always had a ridiculous ending that took me right out of his stories. He never seemed to be able to keep the horror aspect rolling at 100%. There was always this 1950s EC Comics or *The Blob* or *The Thing* camp element to his fiction that was more amusement than fright, and in my humble opinion, was the reason most of his books ended up failing as movies. Your own mileage might vary.

On the other hand, Clive Barker got it, and Clive Barker on film was horrifying. His *Hellraiser* presented a version of evil that had never been explored before. This was beyond the Old Testament vision of Heaven and Hell. Gone was the iconic and clichéd satanic imagery, and in its place, was something a whole lot more terrifying – an underworld with no internal morality or logic. It was damnation anarchy. That made it unpredictable, and the good guys weren't necessarily going to win the day.

Two other films have also imprinted true horror on my psyche: the first would be Ridley Scott's *Alien* that was, at its core, *Jaws* in space; A crew of astronauts discover an alien life form, bring it back on board their ship, where it proceeds to kill them one-by-one. Sigourney Weaver's astronaut character, Ellen Ripley, takes Roy Scheider's Sheriff character, Martin Brody, and turns the tables – making her the predator and the alien her prey. It's a theme explored in more detail in James Cameron's sequel, *Aliens*.

Finally, the film that has stayed with me the longest, and still haunts me to this day, is a low-budget Canadian film called *The Changeling* starring George C. Scott. The film is about a man who loses his family in a car accident and attempts to work through his grief in an old house that has a malevolent secret. It's old-school suspense – more thriller than horror – and is low on clichés and high on spine chilling revelations. The direction makes the film, and simple things like music, ethereal sound, and lighting become hair-raising effects. It will make you believe in ghosts. Something I do not in real life.

But there was that one time…

CHAPTER TWO

DOWN THE MISSISSIPPI DOWN TO NEW ORLEANS

When my wife, Sharon, and I first got together I decided the sure-fire test to see if we were compatible was to travel together. If you can't spend three weeks on the road, in a car, living out of suitcases, and sightseeing together – you shouldn't get married. To me, a long distance trip is a metaphor for everything good and bad that could be hurled at a relationship from budgeting money, to enduring weather, to fighting traffic jams, to sleeping in a different bed every night, and to compromising on what direction to go. Yes, I do have a keen sense of direction until getting lost in the rain in a bad part of New Orleans at which time I *do* ask for directions!

So, in October 1994, we packed up my two-door Chrysler Turismo hatchback, and headed to the U.S. of A. It was a cross-America sojourn from New York to L.A. just like Patsy Gallant sang about in 1977. We were on the road for 22 days, and covered 11,000 kilometres, and even hit Las Vegas in time for Canadian Thanksgiving where we managed to find a buffet-ready turkey dinner-for-two at the Riviera Casino.

Of course, there was an obligatory stop at the Grand Canyon, the Carlsbad Caverns in White City to watch the bats, New Mexico, and out to Los Angeles to visit the Queen Mary, and Universal Studios. On the way back east, a State Trooper stopped us for speeding. I was coming out of a very dangerous hill from the Hoover Dam because an 18-wheeler was attempting to race us to the bottom a la Dennis Weaver in the movie *Duel*. The trooper saw that we were from Canada and sent us on our merry way with only a warning and a concerned "be safe."

The highlight of the entire 22 days, however, may have been New Orleans. We didn't spend a lot of time there, but managed to hit several sites mentioned in Anne Rice's *Vampire Chronicles* books, and the '*Witching Hour*' – the cover of which features the entranceway to the cemetery up the street from her house.

We found her house in the Garden District not far from the homes of producer Daniel Lanois and Nine Inch Nails front man Trent Reznor. We even posed in front of the spooky antebellum home where her husband was home that day. We didn't have the nerve to knock on the door, but did end up at a book store not far away where Rice frequently stopped in to autograph copies of her titles for tourists like us.

It was a phenomenal trip all round. Sharon and I established that we were more than compatible to travel together, and maybe getting married might be a neat-o idea.

JAIMIE VERNON

THE HONEYMOONERS GO TO HELL

So, on March 15th, 1996 we tied the knot in Markham, Ontario, and had our reception at the West Rouge Community Centre where we had a Rock and Roll reception. The event featured a DJ, and live bands that included many of our musical friends who got up and performed. Sharon and I then went to the former Renaissance Hotel to stay before heading out for the honeymoon the next day. Instead of having sex that night, we rolled around in all the money we got as gifts. It was going to pay for our next adventure.

The following morning the car wouldn't start. It was well below sub-zero as any idiot getting married in Canada in the winter could have told us. We got a boost, did a few errands, and went on our bleary-eyed way. It was a portent to trouble down the road - literally.

The plan was to return to New Orleans directly where we could spend at least one night on Bourbon Street, and the remainder out in Harvey, Louisiana, where it was quieter. However, we soon found ourselves stranded in Franklin, Kentucky, with a completely dead battery at 6PM on a Sunday night. Unbeknownst to us, they apparently rolled up the sidewalks, closed the bars, and shuttered the windows so that the *Children of the Corn* were less likely to kill the denizens of this quaint little Mayberry town in their sleep.

With that issue, we also couldn't get anyone to give us a boost, or tell us where one might find a simple amenity like a gas station, or a tow truck. It was like we were on the abandoned town square set of *Back to the Future* where Marty McFly lands in the 1950s. It was dead quiet and lifeless.

Finally, we found a guy sweeping up his pool hall/bar and reluctantly gave us a large Styrofoam cup full of water to put in our car's dried out battery. We needed more water. The battery was bone-dry. Luckily, there was a water tap outside the Town Hall/Library to give us more, but without a boost we were going to be sleeping in our car in the Town Square regardless. Knocking on doors of the surrounding houses didn't seem safe as both of us sported very long hair and black leather jackets. We were the invaders in Anytown, USA in an episode of the *Twilight Zone*, it seemed.

A walk to a self-serve gas bar found us talking to a young gal whose "Y'all's" were mighty thick. Her tow-trucking brother/cousin/boyfriend (most probably one and the same guy) was too far out of town to assist. Fortunately, the bar-owner guy stumbled by while dropping off mail at the post-office next door, and he saw that we were still stranded. He hesitantly drove us back to our car, helped with a boost, and offered to find us a B & B to stay at for the night. Except that our car no longer generated enough power for our headlights to function properly and we lost him at a forked road in the dark.

He went one way, and we decided to take our chances instead by heading back to the highway where we'd originally detoured, and began a search for amenities like a garage or hotel. Like lighthouse in the dark, we found a Holiday Inn Express with a very friendly Pakistani gentleman who hooked us up with a room. The car could wait until the morning as we were exhausted. We spent the evening rebooking all our hotels for the rest of the trip, and finally went to bed.

I looked through the motel's Yellow Pages directory

in the morning (that's a phone book to all you young kids out there), and the day-shift manager helped direct us to an Auto Zone dealership – ironically, just a block from where the "Y'all" gal's gas bar was. I went in to the store and sidled up to the battery counter – yes, they had an entire *department* of nothing but batteries.

The deep-fried Southerner behind the counter asked if he could help me.

"Yes, I want the highest cold-cranking amperage battery available on the planet."

"Are you driving an 18-wheeler semi-rig?"

"No, I'm from Canada. This thing has to turn over at –40 Celsius."

"Canada? Wow. You're a long way from home! Here. We have this Forever Ready Kick-Ass Voltage Morpher 1500 with Bun Toaster and Curling Iron on sale. It should get you through any winter weather. It has a 5-year warranty. If it dies before that, just bring it back, we'll replace it for free."

"Take no offence, kind sir, but I never plan on coming back to this town ever again. How much is it? I only have about $200 to spend."

"None taken and it'll be $98. We'll even install it for you at no charge."

And with the transaction complete, the store's bus boy, Jethro T. Humdinger, brought the battery out to the parking lot and had the car fixed up in about 9 minutes flat. Before he'd even slammed the hood shut we were on the highway, and miles away waving at them in the rear view mirror with the music from *Deliverance* echoing in the distance.

We made it to New Orleans as planned via a trip

down the historic Natchez-Trace Parkway. It's an amazingly pristine paved road through 444 miles of untouched forest where early settlers on horseback and in stage coaches traded goods as far back as the early 1800s, but was originally home to the Choctaw and Chickasaw native Americans for nearly 2000 years before that. The road leads squarely into Natchez, Mississippi, with some of the most awe-inspiring antebellum homes in existence.

THE GHOST AND MR. CHICKEN
We finally made it to New Orleans where we did something truly odd for two honeymooners. We went on both a cemetery tour and a ghost tour. It was our sole purpose for going as we'd fallen in love with the atmosphere of the entire place during our 1994 trip. The city is recognized as one of the most haunted in the world because its history goes back more than 400 years.

Our first outing was through Hauntings Today Ghost Expeditions. Our tour group started out on Toulouse Street with a very enthusiastic woman who was both historian and ghost story narrator. It was quite entertaining as we were led into a bar in the French Quarter that was home to crooner Harry Connick Sr. - father of Harry Connick, Jr. – the Singing District Attorney. I was fascinated by the age of the bar – wooden floors and brick walls – and tried my best to engage in the tall tales that the woman was telling our group about its haunted history.

Though I'm a skeptic, Sharon believes she heard something echoing in the room and I have no reason to doubt her. The tour was going to get progressively weirder for both of us.

Off we went to a courtyard that backed onto O'Flaherty's Irish Channel Pub presumed to be the most haunted place in New Orleans. History shows that in 1806 a Mary Wheaton married her third husband, Joseph Baptandiere, and with her considerable wealth opened a feed store at 508 Toulouse Street. They lived upstairs in one of the building's many apartments. Following the hiring of Angelique Du Bois to help run the store in 1810, Joseph and her began an affair. Over time, Angelique began to get tired of playing second fiddle to Mary, and insisted that Joseph divorce his wife to marry her.

Joseph, clearly enjoying his wife's wealth and some action on the side, resisted the idea. Angelique made it priority number one and many arguments ensued. One day their argument became physical and Joseph tossed his mistress from a window in the apartment she shared with Joseph and Mary in the same building. Her neck broke when she hit the cobblestones in the courtyard below. Joseph rushed immediately to clean up the blood, and stuffed the woman's body down a sewer hole in the courtyard.

But as he was hiding his murder victim, Joseph noticed a young boy looking at him from a window in another apartment above. Fearing he'd be found out for both the affair and the murder, he ran to his marital apartment on the second floor and hung himself from a window.

Saddened, but not distraught by the turn of events, Mary continued living in the apartment while still running the feed store until her own death in 1817.

Paranormal investigators have made a point of visiting this spot for years in hopes of corroborating the many ghostly sightings of the members of this love triangle. While we were there Sharon took part in an exercise with other group participants to check cold spots by a tree in the courtyard. This is where it is believed that Joseph dumped Angelique's body. Sharon felt the cold spot. I ran my hand over the area as well, but felt nothing. Joseph's spirit, allegedly, was known to buzz around anyone entering the courtyard or the gift shop that was attached.

Within minutes of being there, Sharon started to feel her ears tingle. We asked the tour guide how Joseph would manifest and she confirmed that tingling skin was common. One of Sharon's ears, and then the other, turned beat red, and were irritated. I started feeling uneasy as if I was going to black out. It was a full-body nausea and the back of my neck started to tighten up like my blood pressure was rising. I started to panic. Something wasn't quite right, and Sharon could see I was a bit spun out.

It took a few minutes after leaving the courtyard for me to calm down, but I never quite shook the feeling of an ominous presence. I wouldn't say it was a ghost, but it was certainly something malevolent. I didn't talk much after that. It was like all the sunshine had been pulled out of my body, and I was just stumbling blindly toward wherever my body led.

Our next stop was Le Petit Théâtre du Vieux Carré that is considered the oldest continuously running community theatre in the United States. Opened in 1916, the building actually houses two theatres – a small one for children, and another for adult productions separated by a large lobby decorated in the fineries of the early 20th Century.

The original building was built in 1794, burnt down, and was rebuilt in 1797, becoming the living quarters for the last Spanish governor of the Louisiana colony, Don

Manuel Gayoso de Lemos. The children's theatre occupies this space. The larger theatre, dressing rooms, and offices were built in 1922.

It is believed that the ghosts of between 11 and 13 people haunt the entire theatre complex. Some are believed to be the spirits of actors whose lives ended tragically. Some are believed to be happier apparitions of children. All I know is that the second we walked through the lobby my single lens reflex camera (remember those?) began to jam as I tried to take pictures. The shutter would close and lock down. I double-checked my settings. They were the same as when I had taken shots in the O'Flaherty's Pub courtyard, but I'd opened the lens a bit wider to take in more natural lighting as the theatre was dimly lit.

As we entered the large theatre, I took a photo from the back doors to get the entire view of the room in one, panoramic, shot. The shutter jammed. The photo that was developed when we got home from our trip shows the tour guide sitting on stage, with a body standing in front of her obstructing the view. Several other photos had unintentional flashes and light leakage across half the images. I have to believe this was an effect of whatever was in the building because the camera never did it before, or ever again.

There's nothing creepier than being buzzed in a courtyard by a 'spirit' and having a perfectly functional camera fail to do its job during a visit to a theatre that has been deemed one of the most populated haunted buildings in the world. I'm still not sure I'm a believer, but the creep factor was extremely high.

DEAD MOZELL & THE MAGIC TOUR

Richard Rochester was the owner of the Dead Mozell Café on Iberville Street in New Orleans. It was named after a famous photograph of a woman named Molly Martin posing with her two daughters Cora Lee, who was very much alive in the photo, and Mozell, who had succumbed to a childhood illness in 1913, propped up mannequin-like. Death photos like these were common place in an era when photos were very expensive and special occasions few and far between. The portrait was life-sized and graced a wall behind the Café's cash register.

Rochester ran the Magic Walking Tours, and specifically, a Cemetery Tour of the burial grounds at St. Louis Cemetery No. 1. It was here that we were introduced to our first taste of a real, historic, cemetery. Unlike Canadian cemeteries, the graves are above-ground vaults due to the unpredictable flooding in the Mississippi Gulf basin. St. Louis Cemetery No. 1 is the oldest of the three cemeteries within the City of New Orleans, and was established in 1789, and occupies eight city blocks. It's located very close to Storyville - the pre-Depression Era slum where music legend Louis Armstrong was born and raised.

The cemetery site is home to Voodoo Queen Marie Laveau, and the soldiers killed in the Battle of New Orleans which, tragically, had been fought after the Civil War had ended, but the combatants hadn't received the news until it was too late. This is also the location of the pyramid tomb built by actor Nicholas Cage which sports the inscription *Omnia Ab Uno* ("Everything From One") featured prominently in Cage's movie *National Treasure*.

Other notables are French-Creole aristocrat and

politician Bernard de Marigny; architect and surveyor Barthelemy Lafon who allegedly became a Jean Lafitte pirate; world chess champion Paul Morphy; and notorious 19th Century plantation slave owner Delphine LaLaurie, who was said to have tortured and killed her slaves. For whatever reason, Nicholas Cage bought the building where LaLaurie allegedly tortured these people. It's any wonder that between the pyramid tomb (which was blessed by a Voodoo Priestess) and this building acquisition, people believe Cage to be part of the Illuminati. He's one strange dude.

But, then again, New Orleans is one strange place.

GETTYSBURG ADDRESSED

One of the members of the rock band Klaatu, Terry Draper, was signed in 1997 to the record label I ran. In 2001, we released two Civil War-themed CDs – one was pop music with a Civil War thread running through many of the tunes, the second was a CD-EP of specific Civil War related songs including Terry Draper's interpretation of "Dixie".

As a marketing and promotional venture, we piled into my van in the dead of summer and decided to hit the souvenir shops at all the Civil War National Battlefield Parks throughout Virginia and Pennsylvania. Terry was encyclopaedic in his knowledge of the battles and the history of the war, and guided our journey through places like Manassas and Gettysburg.

Gettysburg might be the most overwhelming piece of vacant land I've ever stood on. The scene was of rolling, majestic green fields that belie the horror that once graced it. Period cannons dot the outskirts of the battlefield and a scenic road allows you to visit the monuments to the thousands of soldiers that died. At the north end is the National Cemetery where Lincoln gave his historic Gettysburg Address.

It's an idyllic arena juxtaposed against so much bloodshed. It is surreal and haunting. Sharon has actually gone on ghost hunts on the Gettysburg battlefield. It would have been interesting, to say the least, though I'm not sure that I wouldn't have felt as ill-at-ease as I did in that New Orleans courtyard. Gettysburg is the largest mass grave in the United States and its energy is one of great tragedy and sadness.

HOLLYWOOD FOREVER

Sharon and I began to visit Los Angeles around 2001 on a semi-regular basis. It was an oasis away from the frantic Rock and Roll lifestyle we'd assumed as my record label, Bullseye, was becoming bigger and more widely known. Our pretence for going was always as part of entrepreneur David Bash's annual International Pop Overthrow Festival. We'd send our artists to Los Angeles to play the festival and tag along as roadies and tour guides.

We are both fans of the TV show *Buffy the Vampire Slayer*, and its spin-off, *Angel*. Much of the exterior fight scenes with vampires and demons were shot around Hollywood – specifically Angelis-Rosedale Cemetery which was used frequently in its plots (pun intended). We took a day trip out one day and wandered around looking at graves. It's a rather young cemetery, in the grand scheme of things, as Hollywood itself is barely over 100 years old.

Noted interments there include most of Los Angeles'

mayors, a few Civil War and World War soldiers including Tuskegee Airman Demmit Charles Griffin I, actor-singer Fernando Lamas, boxer Henry Armstrong, Baseball Hall of Fame athlete Frank Chance, the daughter of insane Russian cleric Rasputin (!!), as well as actors Everett Sloane (*Citizen Kane*), Ernestine Wade and Tim Moore (both of *Amos 'n' Andy*), Dooley Wilson (*Casablanca*), the first Chinese-American actress, Anna May Wong, plus Hattie McDaniels and Ernest Whitman (both of *Gone With the Wind*).

We got a real taste of the famous and dead, but wanted to see more. We had become tourists of the moribund. On a return trip in 2006, we expanded our cemetery touring to include the better known Hollywood Forever and Westwood Village Memorial Park Cemetery.

Hollywood Forever is the only cemetery in Hollywood proper, and was originally known as Hollywood Cemetery when it was established in 1899 by developers Isaac Lankershim and Isaac Van Nuts. After selling off a portion to Paramount and RKO movie studios by 1920, and the setting aside of Jewish burial land under the name Beth Olam Cemetery, 51% of what was left was purchased by convicted felon and millionaire Jules Roth in 1939 because his parents had been interred there. Roth renamed the cemetery Hollywood Memorial.

The problem was that Roth used the proceeds from the cemetery to continue living his hedonistic lifestyle and allowed the cemetery to fall into disrepair. In 1974, the crematorium was shut down immediately after the cremation of Mamas and Papas singer Cass Elliot when the furnace bricks collapsed on top of her casket during the proceedings.

In the 1980s, Roth also began selling portions of the cemetery off to developers to put up strip plazas in an effort to pay off back taxes to the city. Following the leasing of an entire roadway to Paramount Pictures for employee parking while their parking garage was being renovated, over 1,000 families with plots there filed a class action lawsuit against Roth for invasion of privacy.

To make matters worse, the 1994 Northridge earthquake left many of the crypts and family vaults cracked and broken. Roth was unable to fix any of the damage as the cemetery was no longer generating sustainable revenue, and he actively took $500 from families to disinter their loved ones to be placed in other cemeteries.

With Roth's eventual death in January 1998, the State of California revoked the cemetery's licence to sell its remaining interment spaces. It was also discovered that the endowment fund used to care for the interred in perpetuity had been pilfered to the tune of $9 million.

A bankruptcy, later in 1998, allowed two new owners to purchase the entire 62-acre facility for a paltry $375,000. The cemetery was renamed Hollywood Forever and millions have been invested in renovating, restoring and bringing respectability back to the property, and allowing the dead to have the respect that Roth had robbed from them.

The list of famous people buried there is remarkable and stands as one of several monuments to the power of the entertainment business over the last century. The names most recognizable to fans of pop culture are:

Don Adams (*Get Smart*)
Charles Avery (an original *Keystone Cop*)

Richard Blackwell (fashion critic)
Mel Blanc (man of a thousand voices)
Charlie Chaplin Jr. (son of silent film star Charlie Chaplin)
Espera Oscar de Corti (aka Iron Eyes Cody – the man that portrayed the crying Native American in several 1970s *'Keep America Beautiful'* PSAs)
Cecil B. DeMille (legendary movie director),
Nelson Eddy (actor/singer)
Douglas Fairbanks (silent movie star)
Douglas Fairbanks Jr. (*Dawn Patrol, Morning Glory, Gunga Din*)
Peter Finch (*Sunday Bloody Sunday, Network*)
Victor Fleming (director of *The Wizard of Oz* and *Gone With The Wind*)
Kim Fowley (Rock and Roll impresario)
Estelle Getty (*Golden Girls*)
Griffith J. Griffith (donator of Griffith Park and observatory)
George Harrison cremated remains (The Beatles…duh!)
Woody Herman (big band leader)
Peter Lorre (*Maltese Falcon, Casablanca*)
Darren McGavin (*Kolchak: Nightstalker, A Christmas Story*)
Maila Nurmi (aka Vampira)
Tyrone Power (*The Mark of Zorro, Witness For the Prosecution*)
Dee Dee Ramone and **Johnny Ramone** (whose ashes are with his wife but will be interred there after her death)
Nelson Riddle (orchestra leader)
Mickey Rooney (*Andy Hardy, National Velvet, Babes In Arms, A Midsummer Night's Dream*)
Ann Sheridan (*Angels With Dirty Faces, The Man Who Came*

To Dinner, I Was A Male War Bride)
Benjamin "Bugsy" Siegel (gangster, founded the first casino in Las Vegas)
Jerry Siegel (co-creator of comic book hero *Superman*)
Carl "Alfalfa" Switzer (*Our Gang, The Little Rascals*)
The Talmadge Sisters (actresses in many silent films)
Toto's cenotaph (the dog from *The Wizard of Oz*)
Rudolph Valentino (*The Sheik, Blood and Sand, The Four Horsemen of the Apocalypse*)
Scott Weiland (vocalist for Stone Temple Pilots, Velvet Revolver)
Hobart Johnstone Whitley (the man that named Hollywood while visiting on his honeymoon)
Holly Woodlawn (Andy Warhol acolyte and subject of Lou Reed's song *Walk On the Wild Side*)
Fay Wray (*King Kong, The Bowery, The Countess of Monte Cristo*)

    Sharon and I were unable to spend more than an hour or two there as the site is so incredibly big. Bigger than Beacon Hill, in fact.

    In contrast to Hollywood Forever, is the Westwood Village Memorial Park Cemetery off Wilshire Boulevard, and is only minutes from Santa Monica in west Los Angeles. The grounds are hidden behind a series of business offices and apartment buildings, and you can easily miss the site if you were to just casually drive by.

    For such a small enclave of graves and vaults, Westwood packs a punch of celebrity names from more recent pop culture. It wasn't always that way. Marilyn Monroe was one of the first celebrities to be interred there because her husband, Joe DiMaggio, knew Monroe's beloved childhood caregivers – Grace Goddard and Ana

Lower – were both laid to rest there. Other celebrities followed suit in the 1960s and it has become its own Hollywood Walk of Fame. Among some of the well known names interred there are:
Eddie Albert (*Green Acres*)
Patty Andrews (of singing group The Andrews Sisters)
Eve Arden (*Our Miss Brooks, Grease*)
Robert Alexis Arquette (transgender entertainer)
Lew Ayres (*All Quiet On the Western Front, Dr. Kildare*)
Jimmy Backus (*Mr. Magoo, Gilligan's Island*)
Lloyd Bochner (*Point Blank, Twilight Zone, The Virginians*)
Ray Bradbury (author of *Fahrenheit 451, The Martian Chronicles, I Sing The Body Electric,* and *Something Wicked This Way Comes*)
Les Brown (big band leader)
Sebastian Cabot (*Family Affair*)
Sammy Cahn (songwriter for Frank Sinatra, Dean Martin and Doris Day)
Truman Capote (author of *Breakfast At Tiffany's, In Cold Blood*)
John Cassavetes (actor, producer, director, *Rosemary's Baby, The Dirty Dozen*)
James Coburn (*The Magnificent Seven, The Great Escape*)
Jackie Collins (author of 32 romance novels), Ray Conniff (band leader)
Alexander Courage (TV and music score composer; *Star Trek*)
Bob Crane (*Hogan's Heroes*)
Rodney Dangerfield (actor, stand-up comedian)
Richard Dawson (*Family Feud* game show, *Hogan's Heroes, Running Man*)
Dominique Dunn (actress from *Poltergeist*, daughter of

crime writer Dominic Dunne and murder victim – California's stalking laws were changed after her murder)
Ariel and Will Durant (Pulitzer Prize winners for literature)
Peter Falk (*Columbo*), Farrah Fawcett (*Charlie's Angels*)
Eva Gabor (sister of Zsa Zsa Gabor, star of *Green Acres*)
Paul Gleason (*All My Children, Breakfast Club, Trading Places, Die Hard*)
Jane Greer (*You're In The Navy Now, Prisoner of Zenda, Against All Odds*)
Merv Griffin (producer, singer, TV show host)
Latasha Hardins (whose murder shortly after the beating of Rodney King was said to be the impetus for the 1992 Los Angeles riots)
Jim Hutton (father of actor Timothy Hutton, *Ellery Queen, Where The Boys Are*)
Janis Joplin (iconic singer-songwriter)
Brian Keith (*Family Affair*)
Gene Kelly (actor, dancer, remains were scattered at sea)
Stan Kenton (influential experimental jazz composer)
Don Knotts (*The Andy Griffith Show, Ghost And Mr. Chicken, Shakiest Gun In The West, The Incredible Mr. Limpet, Three's Company*)
Burt Lancaster (*Elmer Gantry, The Birdman of Alcatraz, Airport, Atlantic City, Field of Dreams*)
Peter Lawford (one of the legendary Rat Pack and John F. Kennedy's brother-in-law)
Peggy Lee (singer), Janet Leigh (mother of Jamie Lee Curtis, *Psycho, Manchurian Candidate, Bye Bye Birdie*)
Jack Lemmon (*Some Like It Hot, The Apartment, The Odd Couple*)
Robert Loggia (*The Greatest Story Ever Told, An Officer and*

a Gentleman, Prizzi's Honor, Independence Day)
Karl Malden (*Streets of San Francisco*)
Dean Martin (singer, actor, one of the Rat Pack)
Walter Matthau (*The Odd Couple, The Fortune Cookie, Grumpy Old Men*)
Elizabeth Montgomery (*Bewitched, The Legend of Lizzie Borden*)
Carroll O'Connor (*The Heat of the Night, Kelly's Heroes, All In the Family*)
Heather O'Rourke (*Poltergeist, Poltergeist II*)
Roy Orbison (legendary singer-songwriter)
Bettie Page (1950s Queen of the Pin-ups)
Donna Reed (*It's A Wonderful Life, From Here To Eternity Dallas*)
Buddy Rich (drummer, band leader)
Minnie Ripperton (singer and mother of actress Maya Rudolph)
Doris Roberts (*Everybody Loves Raymond, Remington Steele*)
Wayne Rogers (*M.A.S.H.*)
George C. Scott (*Patton, Firestarter, Dr. Strangelove, The Changeling*)
Sidney Sheldon (mystery writer and for TV shows *The Patty Duke Show, I Dream of Jeannie*)
Robert Stack (*The Untouchables, Unsolved Mysteries*)
Dorothy Stratten (murdered Playboy model)
Mel Tormé (legendary crooner)
Ray Walston (cremated, *My Favourite Martian, Of Mice And Men, Fast Times At Ridgemont High, Picket Fences*)
Billy Wilder (movie director *Double Indemnity, Sunset Boulevard, The Seven Year Itch, Some Like It Hot*)
Carl Wilson (member of pop group The Beach Boys)
Natalie Wood (*Miracle On 34th Street, Splendor In The Grass,*

Rebel Without a Cause, West Side Story)
Frank Zappa (renowned musician, composer and social activist)

I came to appreciate not just the legacy of the people buried in the Hollywood cemeteries, but the rich lives we all lead until our deaths. Some just have more fame and it doesn't negate what we all contribute while we're here.

I believe I brought that respect and pragmatic approach to my job as Cemetery Cop when I put the uniform on for the first time in September 2014.

CHAPTER THREE

A MAN IN UNIFORM

I never much cared for wearing a uniform. It felt like a costume and I'm not a cosplay guy. I understood the necessity for it in dealing with the public. It's a passive-aggressive warning sign that someone is in control and doubles as a security blanket for those in need. It projects authority even if those of us wearing one had none. I couldn't so much as write a ticket for loitering, never mind arrest anyone. I don't like business clothes of any kind. They cramp my style, not to mention my underwear, and require a level of care and attention my slovenly personality is repelled by. It means I'm someone's work bitch. Some use the uniform as a personal power trip; I don't have that particular personality disorder.

I prefer casual. Very casual. Wal-Mart pyjama bottoms and a sleeveless T-shirt are about my speed. It's got me into a few awkward workplace situations including the cemetery gig. I spent 15 hours a day in a patrol car. My interaction with the public was less than 3 or 4 of those hours, but I was expected to have a pressed white shirt, black pleated pants, black loafers, a black tie, and shoulder epaulets with a hat of my choosing. I wore a black baseball cap with the security company logo on it. I still wear it. I had to return everything when I left the security company. They let me keep the hat.

It also meant having that shirt tucked in and buttoned up along with my pants. Both were battles against the laws of physics given my rapid weight gain after having been active at my rail yard job the two years previous. I also have one leg shorter than the other – meaning, I'd wear the cuff of my pants out in short order - along with the heel of my shoe from a bum knee caused by a near crippling at the age of 14 playing house league hockey.

And then there was the daily shave. I get 5 O'clock shadow twice a day. It is the bane of my hairy existence. As noted earlier about having blood clots as a baby, I was gifted a massive cranial scar that goes up one side of my head in front of my ear, across the top, and down the other side just in front of the other ear. I could never have a standard brush or cropped haircut as a kid or the scars would show. My hairdo of necessity for most of my childhood was that of Moe Howard from the Three Stooges. This was another contributing factor in my weekly beatings at school.

However, it suited me right through my days as a punk rock musician in bands, but as the 1980s raged, and the mullet became fashionable, I grew it longer for the synth-pop and hard rock acts I performed in.

I was constantly running afoul of the security company's Human Resources officer over all of this fashionista stuff including the length of my hair, which I had cut to collar length as per company policy. She was the worst H.R. officer I've ever dealt with – a bully and a cheapskate. Getting clothes from head office (i.e. her) meant paying the company nearly triple what you could buy clothes for at retail. But given our ridiculously long hours, shopping for clothes like a normal human being was impossible. She didn't care.\

Most days I showed up at the security office and headed straight to the first floor to pick up my assignment kit, keys and radio. I could usually get to my car and take off on patrol before anyone was the wiser. But some days it was necessary to go into the office and clarify notes left by guards from previous shifts or corporate memos from the office administrators. It meant being in the visual line of fire of this woman's office. She'd immediately beeline towards me and gave my appearance the once-over. She'd find something she didn't like about me each and every time, and so I was classified as 'uncooperative' and cited for my sloppy uniform attire. This was a complete contradiction to the reports filed by my field supervisor who'd come visit me on a regular basis at Beacon Hill. He stopped in unannounced to check on my incident reports and my uniform as per the H.R. department's insistence.

Vincent was a bad-ass pitbull-of-a-guard who had worked his way up from the field to mobile supervisor. He wore a black ops uniform, and Kevlar vest, and frequently had one of the company's guard dogs in his patrol car. His reports back to head office were always glowing reviews of my appearance, my report writing skills – I excelled at handwriting – and the positive feedback from Beacon Hill's own staff. He loved me. My wife always joked that he had a 'thing' for me. I can't say she was entirely wrong.

Vincent was usually the liaison on the large funeral details we had to do when traffic control at the cemetery was overwhelming for just one guard. He presided over the funeral of the Brigadier-General that was interred in the fall of 2015 when the sniper team and the bomb squad were deployed (see Chapter 7 of *Tales From a Cemetery Cop*). He offered great advice, and knew the cemetery as well as anyone.

He once related a story of the time he was called to Section 2 where the water shut off valves were for the cemetery. It was a large in-ground vault where weekend grounds keeper Lopez, and me, had won a battle against a near flooding one Sunday. Vincent was called to that entranceway by two of Beacon Hill's site managers to discuss the plans for patrolling the cemetery on the occasion of Hallowe'en. As they were talking, they managed to position Vincent in front of the lid of the vault that was flush to the ground. Suddenly, a hand came out and grabbed him by the ankle. Being a guard with years of training in self-defence, he spun around and kicked at the spot where the hand was. It was another ground worker who was hiding in the vault as a Hallowe'en prank. The man's hand was crushed by the weight of the vault lid as Vincent jumped on it. The man ended up with three broken fingers.

No one screwed with Vincent. He was from the Beacon Hill days when Doberman Pinschers were used as deterrents for those who dared to stay in the cemetery after all the gates had been closed at night. Back then, the neighbourhood was a lot less gentrified and upscale than it is now. It attracted the homeless, the criminal, and the activities of bored teens, and those looking to hide sexual trysts. It was also early days for the security company, so they felt the dogs were a good calling card for enforcement. That idea ended not long after the lawsuits started. The dogs would actually chew on people after chasing them in the dark across the greenery and between headstones. It became a scene of true terror for those unlucky enough not to make it over a fence to safety.

The City of Toronto enacted a no-dog bylaw right around the same time, so the Dobermans were relocated to various factories, car dealerships, and construction sites, around town to deter thieves from stealing supplies. Vincent usually stopped by to see me on his way to delivering a dog or two for overnights out near Pearson Airport.

THE SCOOBY MOBILE

I was unfortunate to get the 'dog' car on most Sunday shifts. It was a station wagon with room for a cage in the back. No one ever vacuumed or shampooed the carpets and it reeked like wet fur 24 hours a day. I always imagined that I smelled like dog on those occasions I was trapped in the car for an entire day's worth of patrols. One of the female dispatchers felt sorry for the guards and attempted to Febreze the car before shifts, but it never helped. It just made the car smell like rotting dog fur covered in lilacs.

Overall, the car was a shambling piece of crap that spewed blue smoke for miles when accelerating uphill. It misfired on five cylinders. Every guard filled the patrol cars up with gas at a station next to the security company's head office. We did it at the beginning or ending of a shift, and the guards that left the cars on empty overnight for us to have to fill early the next morning were the worst kind of scum. After I filled up and headed out to the cemetery one day, the gas attendant called the police to report the car. He thought it was on fire. The company was forced to take it off the road.

But not before the time on Mother's Day when I popped into a nearby McDonalds to grab a meal before my shift started and I hit an old woman's car while she was racing through the parking lot. She was late for church and passing behind me like a bat out of hell while I was pulling out of a parking spot. The blind spots on the station wagon were ridiculous and I didn't see her at all. My back bumper caught the wheel-well on her car as she passed and peeled the front fender so far back that it sardine-canned across the passenger door of her car. I could see the engine block through the rip in the metal.

She got out of the car, apologized, and I went to get my report documents out so we could exchange info. I got in the car to call my dispatcher and notify him when I saw out of the rear-view mirror that she was getting back in her car. I leaped from my seat to catch her, but by the time I got as far as my back bumper, she'd already manoeuvred around my car and taken off. I got the plate, the make, the model, and the year of the car and called dispatch. Those two years I'd worked as a car jockey for CN Rail had paid off. I could identify cars in a pinch by sight. I waited a bit for her to comeback as I ate my breakfast. She never returned, so I headed to the cemetery to start my day.

The station wagon had a large dent where the corner of the bumper caught her car and some paint was scraped off. Very little damage to my vehicle considering what had happened to hers. I assumed dispatch called 911 to report the hit-and-run, but I never heard any follow up. I had more than expected that I would be hauled into head office and reprimanded for backing out of the spot blindly, but I never got so much as a notification about the incident. I suspect what actually happened was that my dispatcher for that day didn't want the hassle of doing any of the paperwork and buried it – including the report I filed at the end of the shift.

SLIP SLIDING AWAY

Fortunately, most shifts involved the use of a big-assed Chrysler on par with any full-sized police cruiser. These were four-door V6's with factory installed stereo system that, considering their use, weren't that bad. Battling with the boredom on patrol was easier when you had CD's to listen to or, at worst, the local radio stations.

The guard that I replaced when I started at Beacon Hill was a nervous driver by all accounts. The cemetery is built on a series of hills including a slowly descending slope toward the cemetery head office when you enter the front gates. During snow storms, Margaret could never get the patrol cars back up that incline and out of the cemetery. It seemed odd to me considering the fact that she could have crossed under a bridge and come out the exit on the opposite side of the cemetery where there were other exits on level ground. All late model Chryslers have Positraction (a mechanical locking differential), but no one ever taught her how to use it to keep the car from slipping, even with the baldest of tires.

On one occasion, the car slid backward as she climbed the incline and ended up on the front lawn of head office, knocking out a bench and a light standard. She left the car where it was and told dispatch that she was trapped in the cemetery. The mobile supervisor couldn't get to her because the snowstorm was so bad and the City had closed all the access roads leading to Beacon Hill. She ended up sleeping on a couch in one of the office conference rooms. The staff found her snoring away in the morning and the patrol car sitting on their front lawn. Surprisingly, she never got fired. She eventually quit after burning out doing the job. It's a common hazard for all security guards.

I was a lot more experienced with snow driving, and especially snow driving in Chryslers. I had been the lead damage inspector and car jockey at a CN Rail yard for Chrysler. The guy that trained me to handle cars professionally was a guy ten years my junior, and he was a monster driver, and incredible teacher. He taught me how to pivot cars out of tight parking situations, blind parallel parking, controlled skids on asphalt, sand, snow and ice, clutch and emergency brake manipulation, as well as breaking into vehicles and starting them up without access keys. The controlled skid training saved my life when I was heading to the cemetery one day.

Beacon Hill Road is just that – a road on a hill so high it sits 500 feet above sea level and allows a 270 degree overview of most of the City below. It's also insanely steep and rolls to various heights for several miles leading up to it until you hit that peak. Down the other side is a set of traffic lights and around the corner is the main entrance to the cemetery.

During a flash squall one day, the roads had become dangerously icy. I climbed one of the many approaching rises and as I rolled across the top for my descent, the patrol car began to slide sideways. The rear end of the car started drifting into oncoming traffic. I flipped the Positraction button and turned into the skid (I know…it sounds counter intuitive). The patrol car righted itself just as a car was approaching me from the opposite direction. My heart skipped a beat.

The ride wasn't over.

I sailed down the hill and back up the second rise where Beacon Hill Road was at its highest. I took it a little slower and the tires started to slip. I took the Positraction off and the car gripped the spotty asphalt between ice sheets. The car made it to the top, and as I began to roll over the hill, the ass-end went out of the patrol car a second time. This time it was unforgiving. The rear end resumed its drift into oncoming traffic and I recovered momentarily, but now the car was picking up momentum. My foot was off the gas and I hit the Positraction once more. Nothing. I could see several cars climbing the hill toward me. I pulled the emergency brake lightly, and then released it, and turned into the skid. The car wobbled and fishtailed, then returned to being perpendicular to the road.

Thankfully, the oncoming drivers saw what was going on and pulled to the curb. I counted six cars as a sailed by them. I could see the panicked look in their eyes. I just shrugged and held on for the ride. I kept the steering wheel pointed toward the skid. It wasn't helping, but it wasn't making it worse. I was a brick on a curling rink hurtling toward the intersection at the bottom of the hill. The traffic light was red. I steered and cajoled the car. It wouldn't right itself.

I blasted my horn and turned on the patrol car's

spotlight as I slid into the intersection. The traffic light was still red as I went through it. Sideways. By some miracle, every car had stopped in all directions. I was facing oncoming traffic. The drivers waited for me to get my bearings and I drove off. It seems I had nine lives that day.

Winter tires were never put on the cars for the entire year that I worked at Beacon Hill. Near the end of my tenure, they did rotate out the cars and gave us sparkling new VW's to drive. I often wondered if they were any better in the snow. I left the job before I could find out.

THAT OTHER CEMETERY

Full disclosure here. I mentioned that I worked the beat of five cemeteries that have been amalgamated and fictionalized in the confines of the Beacon Hill stories. Technically, I've only recounted stories from four of those locations for you. The fifth cemetery was an independent contract that I patrolled infrequently. I only worked it when pulling a Friday shift because the gates needed to be locked by our security company at sundown, as Saturday was the Jewish Sabbath.

It was a Jewish cemetery and we'd duck out and close it at dinnertime from our regular patrol route.

The cemetery was long and narrow and the grave markers are lined up only feet apart. When I was a kid, my parents told me it was because people were buried standing up. It's an urban myth. The graves in this cemetery are tightly packed because of the cost of real estate in the neighbourhood it sits in. The cemetery is full and doesn't take any new interments so visitors are the only concern there.

Staff opened the gates weekdays and closed them before they went home except Fridays when they'd bugger off and need us to close them. My first visit was the only interesting visit I ever had there.

This cemetery was the length of a suburban street and a block wide. There were gates at both ends – one that was accessed from a major road, one that was accessed from a back road. Those were easy to close and lock. I called dispatch and told them I'd locked both gates and was heading back to my regular patrol.

"Both gates? There's 20 gates there. You sure you're at the right cemetery?"

I gave him the address and the cross roads. "I've locked the front and the back."

"You need to close the gates on the side street. Go take a look. Some of those gates should still be open."

The road on the long side of the cemetery had 18 gates – one every nine feet. It rivalled Beacon Hill for the number of padlocks that had to be secured. This wasn't wrought iron either, but chain link with industrial strength gates that you'd use to keep people out of a hydro vault or from falling into a pit at a construction site.

At Beacon Hill all the padlocks were cut to a single master key. It made accessing them quick and easy. There was no fumbling with other keys. The front and back locks at this cemetery were newer and cut for a one-key operation as well. However, the side street gates contained 18 individually keyed locks. The key ring I was given had 25 keys on it. None of the keys were marked. It was supposed to be a ten-minute job. It took me an hour. It was an hour that I wasn't on site at my regular cemetery to patrol.

Beacon Hill's assistant supervisor, Mark paged me while I was at the Jewish cemetery. I was reprimanded for being off site for more than my allotted time. Turns out Beacon Hill didn't know the security guards were ducking out Fridays to lock up this other cemetery. I took the hit and didn't say a word. The last thing I needed was to get fired for pointing out that my employers were double dipping.

CHAPTER FOUR

THE WINTER OF MY DISCO TENT

The gates at the cemetery were not particularly co-operative when the weather dipped below 4C. Between that temperature and 0 C, the damp air made for an icy, arctic freeze of the padlocks and the plastic covered steel tensile wires they secured (imagine modern bicycle locks). There were a dozen formulas that guards had for thawing frozen locks, not the least of which was letting the heat from the patrol car's muffler warm them up. The idea was ludicrous and time consuming. When you needed to get dozens of access gates open in 30 minutes you had zero time to waste hot-venting a padlock. More problematic were the gates located on pedestrian pathways where you couldn't drive a car.

I carried a kit containing WD-40 and a squeeze bottle of lock de-icer with me. Breathing on the locks also worked when all else failed. I imagine it looked rather indecent for someone passing by while I was bent over blowing on the gates.

After opening them, the guards with the least amount of ingenuity would leave the locks and the steel wires attached to the gates during bad weather days, and would be stuck thawing them out again at closing time. This caused two problems. One was that passersby would occasionally steal the locks and the wires. The other was that the temperature almost always plunged by nightfall, making the locks impenetrable with a key regardless of WD-40, locks de-icer, or a Bic cigarette lighter.

I had a solution that ended up being adopted by all the guards. When I opened the gates in the morning, I'd take the locks and the wires off as I freed them from the ice, and left them in the warm patrol car all day. At closing time I didn't have to battle any of the headaches when locking up. I had toasty padlocks to put back on the gates. No muss, no fuss.

The fact that guards who had worked the cemetery for years never did this prior to my arrival shocked me. I would have expected that every quirk and inconvenience of the cemetery procedures by security would have had its own tried and tested solutions. I presumed wrong. Critical thinking didn't appear to be in the job description. That's not to say these guys were stupid, they just didn't seem to work out methods of making their work days easier. Maybe wrestling with frozen locks was a challenge to them. It was a pain in the ass to me and I was quick to erase the problem from my daily routine.

The entire grounds were supposed to be open and accessible by 7AM. It was incumbent on me to make sure all the public access gates were unlocked and ready for foot and vehicular traffic. Snow became problematic, not just for me in trying to get to the gates, but for the cemetery's ground staff. They generally arrived around 6:30 AM when I did. I'd let them in the front gates and they'd head to any one of the many utility yards *if* the roads were accessible.

When it snowed, that plan went to hell in a hand basket. If snow was piling up to the bottom of the patrol car doors, staff vehicles, hearses, and procession cars during funerals were going to have a tough time navigating the miles of roads inside the cemetery. I had to hold the line and keep the main gates closed while the early ground staff got the ploughs out to clear the entire cemetery. That job took a good hour, and I was required to hang out at the front of the cemetery and only allow access to the remaining office staff starting work at 8AM.

There was never a snow day closure when I was on duty. Billy, the guard who initially trained me for the job, told me about a winter where the snow was so bad on Beacon Hill Road that the city snowplough couldn't even clear enough room to access the front gate. The snow was over 12 feet high and six feet deep. It was impassable. No one was getting in to the cemetery that day, not even the dead.

Once the roads inside were cleared, it was still a slog. The pedestrian pathways didn't get cleared immediately. Those would have to be shoveled by hand by other grounds staff as the day wore on. First thing in the morning, I had to crawl through it to get the gates open for the one or two die-hard area residents who insisted on cutting through the cemetery. It required heavy boots, and getting one's pants soaking wet.

The worst was opening the gate behind the Visitation Centre. I could drive up to the front doors, and pull into the handicapped zone, and park my car but would then have to jump a hedge, trudge across the V/C's back lawn, and across a bike path to get to the gate. If my feet didn't get wet, my crotch did while attempting to step over the hedge. I was about an inch too short to clear it effectively.

DIG ME NO GRAVE

The only upside to all of it was that the cemetery was usually quiet when the flakes were flying, or when it was a cold, windy day. Gravestones are eerily beautiful when they're blanketed in white. The names are obscured and the smaller stones appear as marshmallow lumps on the horizon. The cemetery sleeps for a good portion of the winter season. There are, however, those who insist on being there no matter what the temperature or the weather forecast.

Many who have loved ones interred will risk their own safety to make their way into the cemetery. It defies logic. The dead are not going anywhere. They slumber through the worst storms year after year. It's all I could do to not shout out "Pick another day" at senior citizens huddled over a tombstone trying to brush away snow as it would continue to fall on their heads. I'd frequently find myself helping them with the lame-ass snow brush we used for clearing the windows on the patrol car.

Others were a little more inventive.

Christmas wreaths are one of the few comforts that the cemetery supplies for those memorializing their family members during Remembrance Day, Christmas, or other relative religious holidays. They stay in place until spring, when family members are asked to remove them from the graves so that spring maintenance can begin.

One afternoon, I drove through a section of Beacon Hill and noticed a woman walking through the snow toward an area that had nothing but foot stones – these are gravestones that lay flat on the ground. She wasn't really dressed for the trek. She had a winter coat on but was wearing shoes, had no hat or scarf, and her jacket was flapping in the −10C breeze.

I stopped and watched her with concern. The whole thing seemed odd. There was almost no one in the cemetery that day, so this lone woman stood out like a sore thumb, especially considering the poor weather conditions. My instincts were correct. She stopped about halfway into the field of graves and began wandering around brushing off the snow while attempting to read inscriptions. Obviously, she was looking for someone's grave marker.

She must have found what she was looking for, and started digging at it with the heel of her shoe. The heel snapped off. She seemed perturbed, but took both shoes off and was standing in stocking feet, pounding at the grave, tossing snow and dirt like a dog digging for a bone. Now my hackles were up. This was clearly not going quick enough for her. She turned to a grave behind her, grabbed a wreath that was propped up on wires, like a croquette wicket embedded in the ground.

Using the entire wreath as an implement, she started

digging again at the grave marker with the wired ends. Again, this was not satisfactory. She started pulling the leaves off the wreath to extract the wires. I jumped out of the car immediately, yelling at her to stop as I ran across the field.

Suddenly, two van-loads of rather large, burly men came at me from out of nowhere, and circled me as I moved toward the woman. One guy took a swipe at me.

I jumped back as he missed and yelled, "What are you doing?"

"She's not harming anyone. Please don't arrest her," one of the other men said.

"Tell her to stop what she's doing. She's destroying someone's property."

We were still about 20 or 30 feet away, facing each other, motionless in the snow.

I counted seven Asian men in trench coats. I kept a safe distance away from them and one eye on her. She had discarded the wreath and now had the ground marker standing on one edge, brushing off the dirt that had been clinging to the bottom of it.

She'd managed to pull this three-foot brass plate out of the ground with her bare hands. I kept one hand in the air directed at the men and used the other to push the emergency alert on my walkie-talkie.

Dispatch answered immediately, "Give me a 10-13." [*report conditions*]

"10-78, dispatch." [*officer needs assistance*]

"What is your emergency, officer?"

I turned to the man and said, "You have two seconds to explain what's going on, or I bring the police in now!"

I radioed back. "10-12, dispatch." [*please stand by*]

The first man stepped toward me again, but I motioned for him to hold his position.

"Please. We mean no harm. She is very upset. She has come in from Taiwan to see her deceased mother for the first time. She does not believe her mother is in the grave."

"You can't go digging up grave markers. That's just disrespectful. How dare she? I'm sorry her mother has died but you just don't do that."

"So sorry. We will take her home. We are sorry. So sorry."

"And have the wreath put back where she got it, too. That's also disrespectful. She has some nerve. Someone else's family is grieving too, and she destroyed their memorial."

"I understand," the man said while looking down at the ground. He walked toward her and spoke out of earshot. He then hauled her forcefully back to his van by her elbow. I could see she was shaking her head and crying.

"Dispatch. 10-22. Please disregard."

"10-4, Beacon Hill."

The lot of them got back into their vehicles and left. I went over to the gravesite and re-arranged the wreath as best I could. It was ruined. Nearby, was the grave marker the woman had up-ended. I placed it back in its original position, noted the name and date on it, and gave it to the staff back at the office. Management ended up tracking the grieving woman's family, based on the grave marker name, and had them invoiced for the cost of a new wreath. They then had to explain to the owners of the wreath, why some woman had torn their decoration to pieces like some mad animal. It was just one more bizarre day at Beacon Hill.

STALLED OUT

It wasn't unusual to have a car battery die every now and then in the cemetery. I had a problem with that the very first time they let us drive the new VW patrol cars. I pulled in front of head office at the end of the night to secure the building and file my report. When I came out to head home, the engine was dead. Fortunately, Vincent was in the area and popped by to give me a boost. It was inconvenient only in that I ended up getting back to the security office to sign-off my shift an hour late. No harm done.

However, on two occasions there were stalled cars that needed a boost.

Unfortunately, my employers failed to supply us with anything like jumper cables or anything useful in an emergency situation like a shovel, First Aid kit, fire extinguisher, or blanket. I'm not sure if it was a liability issue, or another example of being too cheap to keep us supplied.

Anyway, the first stall was an older model GM van that had been converted into a wheel-chair accessible vehicle for an old couple who were at head office to do some pre-planning for funerals, hopefully, far in the future. It was already dark, and the gentleman had come out to fire up the van and get it heated before fetching his wife, who had the mobility issues. Alas, the van wasn't turning over. The assistant manager called me to see if I could help. I drove over to check the situation, but I had no cables. We spent ten minutes ringing up the staff members who were still on site until we found someone that had a set. I went and retrieved the cables.

I brought them back for the old man a few minutes

later. He swiped them from my hand in a huff.

"I'm not impressed with the service at this cemetery. First you have the nerve to try to take all our money for the plots we bought, and now you can't even give us a boost right?"

I was at a loss to respond to him. He wasn't wrong, but it wasn't my cemetery and it wasn't actually my job to boost his car. I technically had the right to just leave him there and have the car towed away at closing time if he couldn't move it. But being a dick would have only gotten me fired. I offered my apologies on behalf of the cemetery, and pulled my car around to facilitate the boost. He banged on the front of the car and I popped the hood. He was testing my patience.

By the time I got out of the car, he'd already put the terminals on my car battery. As he turned and walked over to his van to do the same, I realized immediately that he had the polarities reversed. If I didn't fix it immediately he could blow both batteries and we'd all be stranded.

He turned to see me re-arranging the cables and scowled, "What are you doing?"

"Double checking the connections."

He raised his eyebrows and turned to put the cables on his own battery. He couldn't reach it. The battery was at the back of the engine compartment, near the firewall. With the suspension elevated for the automated wheelchair accessories, the van was too tall for him. He looked defeated, and let his guard down. The red and black cables in his hand touched momentarily and sparked, scaring the crap out of him. He dropped the cables on the ground and they shimmied and sparked.

I walked over and put one foot in the middle of the

cables to stop them. Then I bent down to untangle them. After picking them up I waved at him.

"Get in, I'll hook it up. You're going to need to pump the gas when I do."

He mumbled, "I know how this works, young man."

I ignored him and reached over to connect the cables to his battery.

"Fire it up!"

He gave the ignition a couple of turns. The headlights flickered for a brief second, and then died.

"Do it again!"

He yelled out his window, "It'll burn out the starter."

"Wait until I fire up my car, then give it another try."

I got in and started up the patrol car. I flicked the spotlight on the roof of my car to signal him. He turned the ignition again and the van started up immediately. I continued revving the patrol car. I looked up and he'd grabbed the cables and yanked them with all his strength from where he stood in front of the van. There was a shower of sparks as he dropped the cables to the ground, slammed his hood shut, got in the van, and took off.

You're welcome, ass-hat.

The second stalled vehicle was a little more complicated to resolve. There is a ravine leading to a valley and a river in Beacon Hill. It's where I'd previously had a staring match with a coy-wolf on a snow bank one winter's night.

The road leading through the ravine has a cul-de-sac at the end. It's a one-way road leading in and a secondary road heading back out. That road went up the opposite side of the ravine and was quite steep. Water run-off from the embankment was unrelenting as the cemetery had no sewer drainage as a means of maintaining the natural setting of the ancient trees and foliage.

On this particular day, the run-off had frozen across the width of the road and down its length. It was a skating rink. The cemetery crew had dropped brine to help melt it, but it wasn't very effective. Having seen the icy effect before, I avoided leaving the ravine via that stretch of road. I'd cheat and go back up the one-way stretch in hopes I didn't meet another car coming at me.

The visitors weren't as savvy or knowledgeable. A woman had taken the icy embankment road in a restored old school Fiat 500F that was stick-shift driven. She got about halfway up the hill and the car stalled out. I suspect she popped the clutch. Restarting meant engaging the brake, clutch, and gearing down again quickly before the car rolled backwards. She didn't manage the transition. When I found her, the car had slid down the hill and partially up the retaining wall where the road curved down the ravine. The front of the car was on the road. The back of the car was about two feet off the ground propped up by a tree trunk. She'd effectively slid up a tree backwards.

She was standing beside the car yelling into her phone when I arrived. I parked in the ravine and walked up to where she was.

"Having some trouble, I see."

She barely glanced in my direction.

"Ugh. I can't believe this. I have to meet a client to show a house. I don't have time for this right now."

I noticed the pantsuit and faux fur coat. She was clearly a real estate agent.

"Do you mind if I try and move the car for you?"

"Sure. My husband took the Jag and left me with this

God-damned antique. It's a piece of crap."

I barely fit in the driver's compartment. It was the same problem that new Fiat 500's had when I drove them at the rail yard. The driver compartment is about the size of the original Mini Coopers from the 1960s. Apparently, Europeans weren't very tall back then.

I put the emergency brake on and moved the stick shift around to get it into neutral. With my right foot on the brake, I depressed the clutch with my left and turned the key. Nothing. I tried it again. Still nothing. I tapped the gas and repeated the procedure. Nothing. It wasn't turning over.

In fact, the car wasn't making a sound. The woman was pacing and still talking on her phone. I opened the driver's door again and the interior dome light didn't come on. I flicked the toggle on it. No change. I shut the door again and pulled the handle for the headlights – it was a long metal bar with a knob on the end. As I pulled it back, it should have transitioned through the stages of all the exterior lights on the car – parking, running, headlights, and with a twist the dashboard lights on the inside should have come on. Nothing.

I got out of the car and waved at the woman.

She looked perturbed. "Well?"

"Well, you've got a dead battery. You're going to need a boost or a new battery. I won't know until we try and hot wire it."

"Are you fucking kidding me?"

She turned and started yelling into her phone again. She was definitely going to be late for her client meeting. I called the office and asked them to send one of the ground crew out with cables. I went back down the hill and sat in my warm car. I continued to watch the woman yell and gesticulate with her arms flailing about in anger.

A truck arrived about five minutes later with one of the lead ground crew guys, Tyrell, who brought a jumper pack with him. It was a large battery with cables attached so you could boost a vehicle even if you had no other vehicle nearby to reciprocate.

Tyrell looked at the car backed up on the tree, then looked at me, and started to laugh. "Here I thought I'd seen everything."

We both walked up the incline together. The woman stepped aside and didn't break from her conversation for even a second.

"Fiats have the engines in the back," I told him.

"No shit, eh? This should be fun."

"That's only half the problem. The battery isn't in the engine compartment. It's under the back seat. That means removing it to get at the battery. The old Volkswagen Beetles were the same. Not the best design idea. They changed it in the '70s. Maybe this is a later model."

I waved my arms to get the woman's attention so I could ask her what I knew was going to be a futile question, "What year is the car, ma'am?"

Her answer didn't surprise me, "How the fuck should I know?"

Thanks. Thanks for all your help. I imagined at that moment that she'd slip and fall flat on her face. My psycho kinesis needed work.

"Tyrell, go around to the passenger side and look under the seats. I'll do the same over here."

He opened the passenger door and kneeled down to get a better look.

We were able to see each other as we looked under the seats from both sides of the car.

"There's a black box underneath the middle of the bench seat in the back. Just like I thought."

"Sonofabitch."

"I'm not tearing this car apart just to find out that the battery is dead. If we were to boost the car we'd still need to push it down off this tree and get it up the hill."

Tyrell scratched the stubble on his chin. "I wouldn't trust a tow truck on this icy hill. I can get the tow-motor from the Section 3 utility shed. It has a winch on it. We can pull it up the hill and a tow truck could then haul it off site."

"Sounds like a plan."

I had to distract the woman again. "Do you have CAA, ma'am? We're going to have to pull the car off the tree and up the hill, and then have it towed to a garage. The battery is under the backseat and will need to be removed by a mechanic."

"Oh, ferfucksake. This is absolutely fucking great. Just great!"

Tyrell retrieved the tow-motor and brought manpower reinforcements. There were now four of us standing around looking at this car stuck backwards up a tree. I should have taken pictures, but I was afraid prima donna lady would have sued the cemetery, or me, or all of us. We grabbed the rear of the car and eased it down off the tree. The guys put the tow-motor at the top of the hill and we fastened a hook underneath the car. It began to slide slightly. Two of us guided the car on the icy slope as the others reeled in the cable. It took about 20 minutes to get it to a clear area at the top of the hill.

To our surprise, CAA was already waiting for us. The woman had at least made the call to save her own ass. She never thanked anyone. She sat in the cab of the tow truck while the driver hooked the car to the back. All in a day's work, Ma'am. Don't worry about us. We're just out here freezing our asses off for you.

CHAPTER FIVE

THE POST-MORTEM CAFÉ

Not everyone that visited Beacon Hill was angry. Most of them were emotionally distraught. The cemetery administration itself was very understanding. Aside from the bone fide help and concern that the staff had for the hundreds of grieving people they'd see each and every week, they supplied free space for support groups to come and discuss grief, and all the coping mechanisms surrounding it.

One such group was called The Post-Mortem Café. I was a little taken aback when they first told me the name. It seemed like a poke at those who might be too withdrawn in their own raw emotions to appreciate what it stood for. Having met the weekly attendees who came for guidance and support, it couldn't have been farther from the truth. The name addressed the reality of these people being survivors and the analytical examination of their grief.

With professional counsellors working in groups, and in one-on-one sessions, it was almost like Alcoholics Anonymous for the grief stricken. The goal was to wean people off sadness, anger, depression, anxiety, and a million other emotions tied up in the loss of a loved one. The purpose wasn't to forget the person who had passed, but to identify and embrace the foreign emotions created by their death before it could consume them.

Some of the participants had been going for years, not because they were still in emotional pain, but to help the newcomers. They were there to assist and walk people toward a better emotional future. It's a long path to healing and requires patience, dedication, and wisdom. If religion was required to ease the burden then so be it, but the services were always ecumenical and bias-free. Death might be one of the few things in life that is universally the same. What we do before we die, and what we believe happens to us after we die, is what sets us apart and defines who we are individual human beings.

So much is entangled in the death process by society in terms of its importance and impact that many survivors lose their path. Not until we can continue to live a happy life and carry the deceased's memory forward, do we truly defeat Death. That concept might be a simplistic viewpoint, but it is the very thing that stops us as a species from becoming consumed with insanity over our losses. To put it another way, The Post-Mortem Café allows people to step outside of themselves again and view the big picture.

The meetings were at night after the cemetery was officially closed, and I would greet the attendees at the front gate, and guide them to the Visitation Centre. Staff would be waiting for them with warm greetings, reading materials, and a spread of cookies, tea, and coffee. The opening service was held in the chapel only because it could seat a large group of people. I expect that those with deep religious leanings felt comforted there as well.

During the two-hour encounter, the facade of a funeral home would quickly evaporate. The building was bright, and inviting, and filled with love. Many friendships were made and people were able to build new relationships on the back of these tragedies. I view that as successful community building and an awakening to those who believe the funeral industry is only a means to make money.

REQUIEM FOR THE MASSES

In the summer, Beacon Hill was also home to free musical concerts out on the Memorial Atrium lawn, or if the weather was unkind, in the chapel at the Visitation Centre. It was a more pleasing use of the grounds than when it was infested with cyclists, joggers, and dog walkers. The concerts were held Saturdays, and usually attracted a few hundred people. It was two hours of, mostly, uneventful traffic control for me.

One of my regulars, an 86 year-old named 'Nosy Nancy', loved to go to the concerts, but had limited mobility with her walker. I'd arrange to meet her at the gates near Section 3. The gates were close to where her house is and I'd deliver her in time to catch the shows.

She'd always say the same thing to me, "I like the string quartets if they're playing the classics but I'm not much for that populist Mantovani or Stockhausen pig swill. Why would I? Stravinsky was still writing masterpieces while I was growing up. I met him once, y'know, at the Russian Tea Room in New York City in 1970. He was a frail old man by then. Died not long after that as I recall. Such talent."

I'd ask her about the trip to New York, and she'd tell me about going with friends and how risqué everyone thought it was that three single women, and one married woman, were tearing up the town. That core group of women had gone there annually starting in the late 1950s. Sadly, she was the only one still alive.

"I cherish those memories, son. It has kept me young in my mind. Las Vegas has nothing on what trouble we could get up to on those trips. I guess they'd have called us bad girls now. Smoking, and drinking, and carousing. If only the hotel walls could speak."

She'd let out a howl and slap her knee, and I would catch a momentary glimpse of an impish gleam in her eye.

She also liked Big Band music, but would never admit it. Her brother had been killed in the Second World War and she claimed the music made her sad, and she hated to be reminded of his death that way.

On those days when the cemetery music selection was Big Band, she'd still show up at the gates for me to pick her up, but then insist we go to her brother's grave instead. We'd drive to the spot and I'd help her cross the grass to his graveside with her walker and wait in the car until she was ready to leave. The grave was on a hilltop overlooking the Memorial Atrium lawn. The music was more than audible as it would waft toward both of us on the back of a summer breeze.

She would sit and talk to him in absentia with her head tilted back and eyes closed. Occasionally, I'd hear her frail voice rise and fall with the melodies of a Tommy Dorsey or Cab Calloway song. I never let on that I knew.

REGULAR AS CLOCKWORK

Much of my interaction with the public happened on weekends, with Sunday being the busiest day. Many people still adhere to the idea of God's Day and so they would generally finish up a visit to church with a requisite stop in at the graves of their dearly departed relatives. It made for very crowded roads inside the cemetery. I've already explained the nightmare of the Ching Ming festivities and observances in my first book. Paying homage to the dead wasn't relegated to one culture or type of person.

The second oldest regular to visit after 'Nosy Nancy' was a gentleman I only knew as Sam. He was 78 and drove a 1973 Plymouth Satellite Sebring Plus. It was a boat on wheels and guzzled about 20 gallons to the mile in gasoline. The car was unfashionably stylish in olive green and a black alligator hard top. That he managed to keep the sunlight from buckling and peeling it off was no easy task.

He sat on a straight stretch of roadway in Section 1 every Sunday around 3PM. He came to visit his long-deceased wife's grave to switch out fresh flowers like clockwork. Over the year that I worked at the cemetery, I managed to catch all the minutiae of his life. He had been a dock worker, a TTC streetcar driver, and a lineman for the Township of Galt (aka Cambridge), Ontario, among many other jobs in his life.

His wife had passed in the 1980s, and he was currently living with his grand-daughter who cooked, cleaned, and worked full-time so they could both carry on with a simple, but fulfilled, life. He was going to leave the house to her when he passed and not to his "good-for-nothing" son. He feared his grand-daughter would cave in and give his son the house. It bothered him quite a bit. His grand-daughter had earned the right to keep the house as far as he was concerned. His son had done nothing but borrow money and never paid him back.

It was a sad statement about so many of the seniors in our society now. There were always vultures waiting for next of kin to pass away so they could lift whatever was left in their bank accounts. Sam had an ace up his sleeve though.

A woman, who was also a regular at the cemetery, had befriended Sam years before. She had died unexpectedly with no living relatives. As Sam found out during the reading of her will, he had been the only friend she had near the end of her life. She left him $250,000 from the estate.

Sam then changed his own will so that this money, separate from his other pension income and assets, could only be drawn on by his grand-daughter after Sam's passing through a bank trust. Should she pre-decease his conniving son, the money would immediately be turned over to a charity of Sam's choice.

DON'T INVITE THEM OUT

One day I got a phone call from one of Beacon Hill's assistant supervisors saying that a maintenance crew had seen an abandoned wheelchair in an old part of Section 3. He wanted me to check it out and make sure someone wasn't lying on the ground in need of assistance or worse.

I drove over, and sure enough, there was a black wheelchair sitting on the open grass among some very old headstones in Section 3. A million scenarios were racing through my mind. Had the person fallen somewhere? Had they hurt themselves on one of the headstones and was bleeding to death? Was it a teenage prank by some of the neighbouring school kids? Was someone having a picnic in the grass I couldn't yet see?

I got out of my car with my radio ready and walked over to the chair. It looked brand new. There was nothing around the chair at all. There was no bag or coat or a cane or anything that might give me a clue as to its occupant. I started a perimeter check by walking around points leading immediately away from the chair and inspected behind dozens of tombstones. There was no sign of anyone. I got back on the phone to Mark.

"Mark? Jaimie. I'm in Section 3. I've found the wheelchair, but not the owner. There isn't even a vehicle over here. It looks like it got here via manual power, but I don't know where the mystery rider is."

"Yeah, that's what the crew had said too. They first noticed it about two hours ago which wasn't unusual to them, but it was still there when they went past it a few minutes ago."

"What do you want me to do? Put it in my patrol car?"

"No. It has to belong to someone. If it's still there at closing time bring it down to my office. It'll get marked with the other lost and found items."

"10-4."

I sniped the position from my patrol car for the next 20 minutes, but no one came and I eventually had to move on to patrol other parts of the cemetery. I made return trips past the spot every hour. There was no change until I went by just as the sun was setting. The wheelchair was finally gone. Mark and I both concluded that someone may have been visiting a grave, got back in their vehicle, didn't realize that they'd left it behind until later, and eventually returned to get it.

It was the most plausible explanation until the day that it happened again. It was fall and the grass was covered in leaves. The wheelchair had returned and was sitting in the exact same spot. I started getting a bit freaked out with visions of that George C. Scott movie, *The Changeling*, turning over in my brain. I sat and watched the wheelchair hoping very much that it didn't suddenly start rolling on its own.

Nothing happened. The wheelchair, again, sat alone in the centre of a cluster of tombstones unclaimed. I drove away in an effort to shake off the uneasy feeling I was getting from it. There is nothing worse than the brain trying to solve a mystery without any clues. This time I drove slowly around the roads leading up to the area of Section 3 in anticipation of finding someone possibly walking for therapeutic reasons where the wheelchair acted as home base.

The pedestrian traffic was minimal because Section 3 dead ends. Anyone entering or leaving had to come past me through the vehicle gates or would be easily spotted entering through the pedestrian walkways. I was stumped and annoyed. It was driving me crazy. I didn't want to have to worry about hauling the wheelchair back to the office as Mark and I had discussed previously.

I drove back around and parked the car. Sundown was coming and the temperature was dropping. If anyone were going to return for the wheelchair it would have to be soon. The air was crisp and I decided to do another perimeter check of the tombstones nearby. This time I noticed that the wheelchair was facing one specific headstone. There were small rocks laid out on top of it and again down at the base. I walked behind it and saw the same thing. I counted 13 stones in each instance for a total of 39. What the hell did that mean?

While standing in front of the headstone, I turned around to look at the wheelchair. From my new vantage point I could see the chair was sitting on top of a large pile of leaves. I could see steam was rising from underneath the wheelchair. My mind couldn't complete the puzzle. What was I seeing?

I walked slowly toward the wheelchair until I was standing directly in front of it and said, "Hello? Is there someone here?"

The leaves started to move in front and below me. Two red mittens covered in reindeers came up out of the ground followed by two arms in a dark brown coat. I jumped back as they proceeded to grab the wheels of the chair and push it backward away from me. A head popped up. It appeared to be a native Canadian woman wearing a knitted wool cap with earflaps and a pom-pom on top. Her face was covered in dirt and leaves. She moved her feet, which were located on either side of mine. She was wearing dark blue snow pants and Wellington rain boots.

I may have peed myself a little, and most certainly made a noise when she immediately spoke.

"Sorry, I didn't mean to scare you. I was meditating."

I stammered out the words, "U-u-nder the leaves?"

"Yeah, it's very peaceful here. I used to just climb the trees and do it from up there…"

She pointed above us. Some security guard I am. Clearly that's where she had been the first time we found the wheelchair. I felt like an idiot but, I mean, really, who the hell would be looking for people in the trees at a cemetery?

"I didn't see you in the leaves. That's pretty good camouflage."

"I don't like being disturbed. I hope I'm not in trouble."

"No. Not at all. It's just that…why are you here?"

"In the cemetery?"

"No. In this specific spot. Are those your rocks on that headstone?"

She smiled and tried to stand up. She was favouring one leg. I offered a hand.

"Thank you. Yeah, um, the grave is of a long lost relative of mine. An uncle, in fact. I'm not from here originally and don't have any family in the city. I have a ritual that allows me to speak with him. I've discovered a lot about my heritage and about myself. It takes a lot of focus and with my bad leg it's just easier to lay down when I'm connecting with him."

"Do you have a ride or something? It's getting cold and dark."

"Don't worry about me. The wheelchair is just a crutch, really. When I get tired I use it. I don't have a problem walking in and out of here on most days. Guess how old I am?"

She brushed away the rest of the leaves, pulled a mitten off, then dug a cigarette pack and lighter out of her pocket.

"Seriously. How old do you think I am?"

It was a trick question. She looked like she'd been dragged through the ass-end of a farm thrasher. I wasn't sure if I was supposed to guess older or younger than 90 years old.

"Umm…I don't know….ah…"

"I'll be 41 next month and *they* haven't killed me yet."

"They?"

"The Spirit walkers in here. They're everywhere, you know. And if you let them get into your head, they'll suck on your soul. Uncle Natal told me how to keep them out. How to fool them into thinking I'm dead just like them. That's part of why I lay on the ground or wherever."

Now I really was getting creeped out. She took a long drag of her cigarette and squinted through one eye as the smoke drifted into her face.

"You guys do good work here. You keep them locked inside."

"What?"

"You know how vampires can't enter a house until the owner invites them in?"

"Yeah…?"

"None of the spirits can leave the cemetery unless

they're invited *out*."

This was a fascinating twist. It was a brilliant theory even if I didn't believe a single word of it, but now I wanted to hear more.

"So when we open the gates every day they don't leave?"

"They can't. The cemetery fence is wrought iron, am I right? Why do you think cemeteries have been putting wrought iron around the outside for hundreds of years? That's like kryptonite to Superman or garlic to vampires. It keeps 'em at bay. They need to be guided to the open gates and invited through. All that "come into the light" horseshit. Almost nobody knows how it really works and so it rarely ever happens, but when it does they find somewhere to haunt. They're lost and angry and shit. You call them poltergeists. Fucking white people and their ghost story shit. They really just want to be put back. They're like cats that can't decide if they want in or out of the house. They feel safer wandering around the cemetery not out in the real world." She nodded at me, "You want a cigarette?"

"Umm…no. No thanks, I don't smoke."

She looked me up and down as I was the squarest individual she'd ever met.

"I better get the hell out of here. The sun is nearly down. I can see those fuckers floating around at night time. It's annoying as hell. They're all bumping into each other and whatnot."

My bullshit detector was going off and she could see the look on my face change.

"I know you don't believe me, honey. That's all right. I wish I didn't know what I know now 'cause this shit has made me certifiable. Can you tell?"

I didn't know what to think. Was this a put on? A delusion that she believed was real?

She folded up her wheelchair and dug around for another smoke.

Against my better judgement I said, "You want a ride out of here?"

"That would be much appreciated. My leg's bugging me a bit today. The food down at the soup kitchen sets off my gout. You know we're not all fucking alcoholics, right? Just living crappy lives."

I presumed she was talking about her native status. I didn't want to get into a political debate about indigenous people getting the short end of the stick given that I was a well fed white guy with a day job guarding dead people all day.

I loaded the wheelchair into the trunk of the patrol car, opened the back door and helped her in. She tossed the half-smoked cigarette to the ground. I picked it up, gave it back to her and motioned for her to get in the car. She smiled and cracked the back window to let the smoke billow out.

I took her around to the Section 3 vehicle gate and unloaded the wheelchair. She tucked it under one arm and started wandering off down the street. She seemed like a harmless, but very disturbed, individual with some mental health issues…or was she?

I hesitated as I went to get back in the car and looked into the blackness of Section 3 behind me.

From down the road I heard her yell out, "Don't do it. Don't invite them to come *out*!"

THE PAUL McCARTNEY CONSPIRACY

A more recent interment at the cemetery is someone with the last name McCartney. I don't know the family. I expect they are one of thousands of families with this very common name. They seemed well off and a woman came regularly to visit the very large oversized monument to place fresh flowers on the plot with regularity. She drove a high-end SUV and wore very fashionable clothes. All this in keeping with the notion that the plot probably cost a lot of money.

While sniping in my patrol car one afternoon at the front gate watching pedestrian and traffic flow in and out of the grounds, I noticed a dishevelled fellow with long hair and a beard pull up next to the woman on a beat up old bicycle. She had just placed some flowers on the grave and was heading back to her vehicle when the man started talking to her. Within seconds I could hear voices raised and she pushed passed the man and got into her SUV and drove off.

The man on the bike noticed me and rode over, I assumed, in an effort to explain what had happened.

"She works for him, y'know," he said without making direct eye contact with me. *Here we go*, I thought. I was bored and figured this would eat up some of my day.

"She works for whom?"

"Paul McCartney," he said. "Paul is covering up all his illicit affairs. He puts his name on all the graves of the women he has left broken and poor. It's his final 'fuck you' to them for having sex with him. My mother was one of his conquests. I have proof he's my father and…"

"What?"

"My mother knew him in Germany before The Beatles

got famous. My birth records show I was born there. But he was clever. The father is listed as unknown, but my mother told me it was him. She kept all the letters he wrote to her after The Beatles went back to England. He promised to send for her, but never did and then he stopped writing. The last letter she got was from Brian Epstein with a cheque for £1000 in 1964. It was hush money."

"So you're looking for child support after 50 years?" I was genuinely interested in seeing how deep this conspiracy theory would to play out.

"More than that. I have been collecting names of all the women he has left destitute or dead and all his *love* children. I want to work with them so we can file a class action lawsuit against him for damages. He needs to step up. He has the money but his people keep blocking me. That woman I was talking to is one of his people. She works for him. He has them all over Canada monitoring and controlling most of the women he's destroyed. All of them are in Canada and are being followed by his agents."

"His agents?" I could sense that the microphone was about to drop.

"Russian spies, of course."

BOOM! There it was.

"Russian spies, eh?"

"Oh, yeah. Just listen to the *White Album*! It's all spelled out in "Back in the U.S.S.R." and "Rocky Raccoon." Go back and listen to the words carefully. He talks about meeting a Russian agent with the code name Rocky Racoon who he asks to take care of all these women. "Martha My Dear" is code for the women. He calls them Marthas. And the "no one will be watching us" from "Why Don't We Do It in the Road" is the Russian agents promising him they'll keep everything hush-hush. They've been here since the early 1970s."

In my head I was rolling my eyes. To the man's face I just smiled and tried not to be condescending. What must misfire in someone's brain to not only believe that someone famous is your father, but that that person is conspiring against you to destroy your life? I'm certain it's not out of the realm of possibility because deadbeat Dads are universal, even rich ones, but the total grasping for affirmative clues to prop up his conspiracy theory was disturbing *and* ingenious. This beat the Paul-is-Dead rumour by a mile.

"So is your name McCartney too?" I asked innocently.

"NEVER! I would never defile my mother's honour by taking the name of this serial philanderer. He is scum and he needs to be held accountable for what he's done to people like us. I wish he was in jail, but there's no court that would put him away. He has *them* paid off as well. He's as rich as the Illuminati and can have people silenced or killed. He had John Lennon assassinated, you know."

I'd heard enough and raised my voice, "Woah! Woah! Woah! Don't even go there."

I was willing to entertain all kinds of wacky ideas, but now he was treading on sacred ground.

"I can prove it," he implored.

"I'm not interested, thanks. I've got to carry on with my patrols. You're free to ride around in the cemetery, but if I see you harassing that woman again I will have you removed. I'm sorry you lost your mother."

He looked me up and down and shot back, "I didn't say my mother had died."

"Then why are in the cemetery at all? If she's still alive then go be with her. If she's buried here I hope you both find peace."

He grunted and went to speak again, but I drove off slowly leaving him with his thoughts. I never saw him back in the cemetery again, and I truly hope he gave up his fool's quest and/or found some professional help with his issues.

CHAPTER SIX

LOST AND FOUND

Beacon Hill Cemetery is a really, really big piece of real estate. It covers several city blocks and contains more dead people than most Canadian cities have living ones. It should surprise no one that people lose things there.

It was perfectly normal to find the lunch boxes and apparel from the part-time students working on the grounds in the summer. Guards would also report finding glasses, phones, umbrellas, and various pieces of clothing (bras and panties seemed to materialize frequently) among other average household items forgotten by visitors. On rare occasions we'd also find shopping buggies which was unusual because the nearest supermarket or department store was well over a mile away.

The most unusual thing I recall was an artificial leg left behind after a Remembrance Day ceremony. No disrespect to the partially ambulatory, but how the hell do you forget your leg somewhere?

Aside from the occasional dog running amok until it could be reunited with its owner, I only found a few items on the grounds in all my travels. There was a local swimming pool and hockey arena across one of the major street intersections between Sections 2 and 3 and I did find a pair of girls' skates one time. There was also the occasional bicycle chained to the outside of the fences in the same vicinity. If a bike was left there more than a few days the cemetery would have the chains cut and the bikes donated to the needy.

There was one item, however, that became a cause for considerable concern. At the beginning of my tenure at Beacon Hill, Canadians were on high terrorist alert after the assassination of Corporal Nathan Cirillo at the National War Memorial, just steps away from parliament Hill in Ottawa. A large military funeral at Beacon Hill for a Brigadier-General shortly after that meant sweeping the cemetery for explosive devices and a massive police presence was employed to secure the grounds during his interment.

We never had cause for concern after that, until the day I discovered an unattended backpack hiding behind a tree at one of the pedestrian gates. It never occurred to me that this was anything more than a student's forgotten carry-all. It was stupid of me to presume it to be harmless. It was in an unusual spot in the cemetery by a retaining wall, where the black ops snipers had set up their lookouts during the military funeral the previous fall.

I waited and watched to see if anyone was going to come back and claim it. No one returned. My Spidey Sense never tingled, but I was uneasy. I called the assistant supervisor Mark and asked what I should do.

"We get backpacks left behind all the time. I wouldn't worry about it. If you're scared I can have one of the ground crew put it in a concrete urn sarcophagus in case it goes BOOM!" He started to laugh.

"You're a funny guy, Mark. If I die I'm coming back to haunt you."

I approached the backpack with caution. Using a snow brush I grabbed from the patrol car, I inserted one end into an opening on top. It was canvas and had pull strings like a duffel bag. I managed to widen the opening so I could take a look inside. There was a MacBook laptop computer inside and a change of clothes. I leveraged the snow brush behind the laptop and moved it from one side to the other inside the backpack. There were economics textbooks and a three-ring binder inside. It appeared that the backpack was exactly as it appeared – the accumulation of things from an average university or college student.

I picked up the bag by a pull string and took it back to the patrol car. I opened the trunk of the car and dumped the contents out. Inside were the MacBook, two textbooks, the three ring binder, a water bottle, some clothes, earbud headphones, a package of half-eaten crackers, and a cheque book.

I picked up the cheque book and in the top left corner was the name, address and phone number of someone. I slammed the car trunk and took off to the cemetery's head office. At the front desk was Emily, who, for all intents and purposes, was the brains of Beacon Hill Cemetery. She was the watchdog and the facilitator and knew everything that was going on at the site all day long.

I had put everything back in the bag and brought it inside with me. "Where are you keeping lost and found stuff, Emily?"

"There's a locked cabinet in Boardroom A. What do you have?"

"A backpack with a very expensive laptop computer inside. But I have a lead on who owns it. There's a cheque book here with contact information at the top. Can you give him a call and arrange for pick-up?"

"Sure can," she said with her usual sunny smile.

She left a message for the owner, and then took me to Boardroom A so I could transfer the bag into Beacon Hill's hands. She opened the cabinet, and inside was a treasure-trove of unclaimed personal effects – including a set of dentures and a sex toy. I signed a waiver showing I'd delivered the backpack and we went back over to her desk so she could make me a copy.

"Does anyone really believe someone will come back for that vibrator?"

"Someone came back and got the *last one* we found. So, yes."

I wasn't even going to ask. Nothing was unusual at the cemetery if it happened enough times.

BILLY GOAT GRUFF

Billy was the security guard that trained me. I got to know him, not in person, but through his legend. When I worked, he was off, and vice versa, so we rarely ever crossed paths. Occasionally, he'd pop by on his day off to say hello to the staff, and would come around to see how I was doing. I was the newbie, and he wanted to make sure that a) the staff was treating me well, and b) that I wasn't fucking anything up.

He'd been a soldier in Desert Storm during the Gulf War. He suffered serious health issues that often kept him off work for long periods of time. He'd been away from the job for nearly a year just before I was hired and was in the middle of another health crisis shortly after I started working there. The staff at the cemetery feared that if the various ailments didn't kill him the work hours at the cemetery would. He wasn't able to handle more than two 15-hour shifts each week because it would take him five days to recover.

The security company rode his ass about it all the time. He was really good at what he did, and the epitome of every security guard training video. He was meticulous and fastidious, and didn't put up with bullshit from anyone. To that end, the security company wanted to rely on him more than he was able to offer. His illness had made him frail and prematurely old. I had assumed he was a senior just trying to put a little extra coin in his pocket on top of his pension. Turned out he was only a year older than I was.

The manager of the cemetery hated him with a passion because he had become a close personal friend with many of the staff members there. This was considered a conflict of interest. Should management ever fire a staff member at the cemetery, it would be incumbent upon us as security guards to escort them off site. Billy argued that being impersonal to the staff would create tension. If he were ever required to escort one of his friends off the property, he could do it with empathy – and would probably get less resistance from someone he could deal with on a personal level. Loyalty and trust is a two way street, and the staff trusted Billy with their lives.

Despite his by-the-book exterior, he was also a big teddy bear. He was my role model and changed the way I approached everything I did. One of those ways was to detach from the emotional and focus on the mechanics of an incident or an encounter. As was explained in *True Tales From a Cemetery Cop that* was easier said than done. You can't stand among grieving people all day long and not get the feels. I am not a heartless bastard, and neither is Billy - despite his best efforts to make people believe otherwise.

WHICH WAY YOU GOING, BILL?

On one of the rare days when I saw Billy on his day off, he arrived at the cemetery not long after I opened up. He was frenetic as I saw him jump out of his SUV and run into the office to see Emily. I pulled my patrol car up and went in to see what he was doing there. I had a suspicion he'd forgotten something. It was not unusual for someone at the cemetery to find the house keys he'd left in a break room or at a work station in one of the buildings. One night, he got all the way home after a shift and had to drive all the way back to the cemetery to get his keys because he'd locked himself out – that was a four hour round trip. I immediately presumed he'd done it again.

"Whattdya lose this time, ya codger?"

"My iPhone. I had it right up until the end of my shift last night. The fucking thing's worth $600 and if the wife finds out, she'll have my nutsack."

Emily burst out laughing, which made me laugh.

"Oh, sure. You two fuckwads can laugh. I like my nutsack. It's the only thing that didn't get blown off in Kuwait."

"Well, Billy, I'll come with you. We can retrace your routine when you started locking down the buildings last night. It's gotta be somewhere."

Emily jumped in. "I'll send an email out to the staff and tell them to keep an eye out for it."

Billy turned on his heel and headed to the kitchen down the hall in the office. He popped back out a few seconds later with a coffee in hand.

"I take it the phone wasn't in there?"

"I didn't look. I just wanted a coffee. My nerves are shot. I gotta find this thing before Mary wakes up. She's gonna call me on it looking for me and I won't be answering it because it's FUCKING LOST!"

"Calm down. We'll find it."

We got into his SUV and headed to the Visitation Centre. We blew into the lobby like Batman and Robin. There the receptionist greeted us. We gave her the whole song and dance about the phone, and then headed to the garage where the hearses were parked.

"I washed the patrol car last night in here. Maybe I left it in one of the hearses."

"What the hell were you doing *inside* one of the hearses."

"They've got the best stereo systems out of all the fleet vehicles. I'm not washing a car without some major tuneage, c'mon."

"Did you wash the patrol car in slow motion and spray water all over your heaving breasts to get rid of the soap? Were you wearing Daisy Dukes?"

"Fuck you!"

We laughed and laughed, but there was no sign of the iPhone.

Next stop was the Gothic Mausoleum. Aside from the utility buildings it was the first building on the grounds that security opened and closed every day. Billy would have started his evening rounds of shutting down the cemetery from here. Public access was through the front doors near the chapel, but our access started through the loading dock where the bodies were brought in for cremation.

Alonso was the staff administrator and undertaker for the crematorium. He was at his desk doing paperwork when we barged in. Aside from securing the doors, and setting the alarms from the loading dock entrance each night, or turning the alarm off in the morning, we weren't supposed to be in there. Ever. Billy and Alonso were good friends, and when Billy wasn't feeling well or tired of chasing dogs and children around the cemetery all day, he'd hide in the break room where he could get a good cup of coffee.

"What's going on, boys?"

"Lost my fucking iPhone."

"Again? Mary's going to kill you."

"Right?"

"Did you leave it in the can?"

"Heading there now."

Off we went, down a long utility corridor and through a set of oak wooden doors, into the witnessing room for families who were there to have their relatives cremated. It was a completely normal looking sitting room with couches and chairs and paintings on the wall and carpeting and, oh, an eight-foot-long stainless steel pedestal with a coffin sitting on it, ready to be pulled by a conveyor belt into a gaping furnace of hell.

Nothing to see here.

An identical set of doors greeted us at the opposite end of the sitting room that led out into the bottom floor of the mausoleum. Directly across the hallway were the men and women's public washrooms. Billy hunted high and low. There was no phone in either. Our jobs require careful searches in women's washrooms as a preventative measure against sexual assault. You can never be too careful.

We headed upstairs from the basement to the main floor and past the chapel to the other public washroom that was an old unisex bathroom built completely out of the same marble interior as the crypts in the mausoleum. There was no phone in the bathroom. Next to the bathroom is the sacristy or vestry. It's a room where a priest or minister can go and prepare for a service in the chapel. It has a chair and a desk in it, and occasionally got used by the janitor to store supplies. I unlocked the door and Billy took a quick look around. I didn't ask him why he would have been in there the night before. I assume it was another oasis to either sleep in or relax. It has no CCTV cameras near it so no one would know he was in there.

We headed through a back door in the chapel and did a quick once-over of the pews to make sure he hadn't set his phone down absent-mindedly while resting. Billy had to rest a lot, poor guy, and he sat down right after we finished sweeping the chapel.

"I feel a hundred years old. I have a lot of energy in the morning, but I need a nap most days now. Don't let them catch you sleeping anywhere on site, man. They'll fire your ass."

"Duly noted," I said.

We headed back downstairs and said goodbye to Alonso. The small utility shed was next door to the mausoleum. It was a short flight up the stairs into the change rooms and kitchen. I took one side of the building and he took the other. We met back at the staircase.

"You see the ghost yet?"

He was referring to what everyone believed was a spirit that turned the motion detectors on in the building every night.

"I don't believe in ghosts, Billy."

"You should. I've seen some horrific shit on the battlefield but there ain't nothing like the shit I've seen in some of the buildings here. I can't say they're ghosts specifically, but the CCTV cameras have caught some weird stuff I can't explain. They only come out when all the lights are off. Go sit in Alonso's office some night after you've locked up the Goth mausoleum and watch the six CCTV video feeds. Pay close attention to the basement hallway between the two fire exits. It's why you'll find the exit doors unlocked sometimes."

I never did look at the video feed. I was always too busy locking up the cemetery. But he was right. The basement hallway fire exit doors were always a problem. Sometimes they couldn't be secured, and the alarm couldn't be set. I once spent an hour trying to bypass the system just to get the alarm to lock-in. I had maintenance come in and look at the door. It was wood and had swollen from the constant moisture in the mausoleum, so they shaved down one side and the alarm strip fit better against the doorframe. Problem solved.

We left the utility building and sat in Billy's SUV. He

pulled out an iPad.

"I have my iPhone GPS synchronized to the iPad. I was told to do it just in case someone stole my phone. I've never actually tried to use the tracking device. I should have thought of this earlier."

I was intrigued. He got on the radio to Alonso who had set the system up for him and got instructions on how to activate it.

"Unless the battery is dead in my phone I should be able to ping it and get a rough location on this map."

"Here's hoping someone didn't find it and walk off with it."

"Shut up, you."

"Hey, I'm just saying…"

He got the iPad's GPS up and, sure enough, there was a red dot flashing on the screen - except it was showing the thing right where we were sitting.

"The phone isn't in this vehicle is it?"

"Wouldn't that be funny."

We both got out and tore apart the SUV looking under the seats and in the trunk. Nothing. We drove around for a bit to see if the image moved on the screen. It didn't. It was still showing the phone in the spot where we were sitting.

"Have you tried zooming in closer on the map? Beacon Hill is big but relatively small when looking at a satellite image."

Billy ran two fingers over the map and zoomed in as close as the image would allow. Now we could see the road detail on the map to within a few feet.

"It looks like the phone is in the ravine! Did you drop it while locking the gate down there?"

"I don't think so. I lock that gate first before sundown, and then do all the others. I had the phone almost until the very end of the night. Then I can't remember what I did with it."

We drove over to the ravine and sat at the end of the road leading into it.

"The phone seems to be closer to this end and not down by the gate."

"I'll get out and walk along the grass, and you follow in the car. Let's see if we can't get a visual on it."

As I got out of the SUV I could hear a dinging noise like when a car door is left open. There was a couple standing on the grass near a grave.

"Hey, do you hear a dinging sound?"

The couple looked at each other and they pointed to a spot on the ground about halfway between them and me. I walked over as Billy followed in the SUV close behind. Sure enough, there, in a small mud trench beside the edge of the road where the grass began to slope up a hill, was his phone pinging loud and clear.

I picked it up. It was covered in mud. I pulled out a cloth that I normally used to keep my glasses clean and gave the iPhone a once-over. I pushed it through the driver's window and dropped it onto Billy's lap.

"Your phone, sir."

He yelled for joy, threw the SUV into park and jumped out. He ran over and squashed me in a massive bear hug. The couple on the grass just stared at us.

"You've just saved my fucking life, man. This phone is my life line. Phone numbers and videos and pictures of my daughter. I don't know how to thank you."

"Just tell me why the phone was in a trench, next to

the road leading into the ravine?"

Billy had to think about it for a minute, "I must have left it on the roof of the patrol car when I was washing it. I didn't want it to get wet. Then I did the ground sweep patrol every hour once the gates were all closed as you do. It must have finally fallen off when I came down here to patrol. Jeesuz. That's a great fucking phone, eh?"

"Billy, you really gotta focus more. That's an expensive gadget to lose."

He went quiet and contemplative, "Having a hard time remembering shit, Jaimie. Little things. I'm like the absent-minded professor. Chemo. Radiation. It's all wearing me down."

"Get some vitamins into you. B-complex stuff. Especially B-12."

He nodded and we headed back to get my patrol car so I could carry on with the rest of my day.

I wish I could say it was the last time it happened. I arrived one morning at the security office to log in and get my patrol car to start a shift, and I found the phone and his sunglasses in the car I was driving. Dispatch called him, and he retrieved his stuff later. It happened again - a third time - when another guard drove over the phone after it had fallen out of his pocket and under the front wheel of the patrol car when he booked off the night before.

Billy left Beacon Hill a month after I quit in September, 2015. I've been told that he's returned to the cemetery part time after yet another round of health scares. Here's hoping he's back to his old self.

CHAPTER SEVEN

VALLEY OF THE DEAD

The spring thaw presents an interesting set of problems at Beacon Hill Cemetery. The site is a series of properties that were annexed over a few decades during the Industrial Revolution and expanded as the city's population grew while the cemetery's owners attempted to predict mortality rates. Part of the annexed property originally contained a man-made lake and a railway bypass.

The lake was drained and the railway dismantled in the early part of the 20th Century allowing the cemetery to re-landscape and add more plot land and mausoleums. What the planners didn't do was adjust for the new watershed during winter run-off or rainy seasons. Very few storm drains exist on the property, the theory being that all water runs down hill and eventually out of the valley that the cemetery sits in.

There's only so much water that the grass can absorb, and with graves numbering close to half-a-million at Beacon Hill that water is generally accumulating in the holes that caskets sit in.

You don't need to be a planning engineer to realize that excessive water is very bad for cemeteries as witnessed by the upheaval at all the Saint Louis cemeteries in New Orleans during Hurricane Katrina in 2005. Coffins were floating through the streets of the city on the back of massive flooding when the levies broke.

Our city has seen several incredible floods in just the last ten years. It's an issue of population growth, over-development, and poor watershed maintenance upgrades. In other words, we've exceeded the absorption rate of water drainage. With buildings and roads and flooding throughout the city it will now be a common occurrence until the schooled Big Brains resolve the issues.

The cemetery is a mini-version of that same eco-system. Heavy rainfall or winter thaw creates a lot of water in a short period of time and there's nowhere for it to go except downhill. Beacon Hill has a lot of hills and a lot of places for the water to pool. The ravine is notoriously bad as the water runs down the valley sides and onto the road. Many days no one could drive through it as the water would be two or three feet deep until it flowed out toward the river past the pedestrian gates at the end of the cul-de-sac. When the water did subside the ground was littered with flowers, small statuary, and other debris from all the gravesites where people had set up memorials. It really did look like a hurricane had swept through the place.

The valley walls also have graves sitting vertically on them. Many people want to overlook the cemetery when they are buried and to have an eternal roost over the world. I never understood the logic, but I guess it's like the same as the people that want to spend all eternity under a shady tree.

The valley graves are a logistics nightmare. A front-end digger with a long arm and large bucket is used to both dig the holes on the valley wall and to put the casket into it. Some are so far down the valley wall that a second digger is used to hold the first digger from behind using only its bucket while the first digger does the rest of the work. You couldn't pay me enough to dangle vertically on the side of a hill in a two-ton construction machine. That's because shit happens.

One of those shit things is that the water run-off eventually erodes the graves on the valley walls and caskets start popping out the side of the hill. Needless to say, the visual is quite unsettling especially when the caskets are upwards of 100 years old and nothing but rotted frame. Occasionally, the bottoms fall out and you end up with the remains of great-great-great-great-Uncle Jack dangling from a tree root or rock formation. The valley wall creates unusual mummifying conditions because it's always in the sun, otherwise the bodies would have turned to dust aeons before.

The digging crew would have to be dispatched to clean up the mess before visitors got freaked out. Wet valley walls equal slippery mud and unstable terra firma. The operation is extremely dangerous. It goes without saying that the construction machines have met untimely ends on more than one occasion. Fortunately, none of the ground crew has ever been injured. Valley graves are greatly discouraged by the funeral staff for just this reason.

THE RAIN ON THE PLAIN GOES MAINLY DOWN THE DRAIN

The area at the Visitation Centre where I needed to park everyday to unlock the pedestrian gate was at the bottom of where the cemetery's lake once sat. It's a beautifully flat paved parking pad at the end of a large parking lot now. Unfortunately, all of the small inclines and rolling surfaces drain toward that parking pad. For the better part of my tenure at Beacon Hill that area was a foot deep with water. A grey water sewer relief line had been installed beside the Visitation Centre garage when the building was constructed, but if maintenance crews didn't empty leaves in the fall from the catch basin, the water would accumulate quickly during rainy days or winter run-off.

It wasn't unusual to see the funeral staff standing outside the garage doors smoking during coffee breaks in boots. Even in the summer. The water never seemed to drain away and the ground crew was often sent out to unclog the catch basin over and over again. It was a poorly designed water flow system. On the days that the parking lot was flooded I made sure to not stop at the Visitation Centre unless absolutely necessary. The visitors weren't as lucky and had to walk around the mess through the ash scattering trail or through some patio doors on the building's opposite side. As far as I know, the problem has never been resolved.

THE GARAGE

Speaking of the hearse garage, it was our job as security guards to ensure that the vehicles were locked at the end of every night regardless of whether they were parked inside or outside the garage. Because the cemetery offered full service funerals, the deceased would be brought in by these cars, embalmed and dressed, laid out in caskets for the viewing and religious services, then loaded back into the cars and driven to the plots elsewhere in the cemetery.

These cars were monster machines and kept in top running order. The cemetery had four of these cars plus a black sedan staff car to transport additional people. Two of them would fit in the garage, and two would be left out in the staff parking area along with the staff car.

On very busy days the cars would be gone for the duration and then be parked haphazardly where security often have to re-park them at the end of the night so we could close and lock the garage doors. It was always a pain in the ass to find out that the keys to one hearse or another weren't located in the staff office on designated key hooks. It would mean a series of phone calls or texts to find out where the keys had gone. We tried to be discreet because many times it was an absent minded staff member who'd accidentally taken them home. Alerting management about the oversight would result in a reprimand. I liked the funeral staff and never reported the error. They, in turn, never reported my errors like times when I'd forget to lock a door in the building or missed setting an alarm.

For the longest time, the traditional hearse was usually a modified Cadillac with a reinforced chassis that can carry up to 1500 lbs. of cargo weight (casket and body combined). In recent years, funeral homes and the cemeteries have begun buying a larger Eagle-class Lincoln MKT built in Brazil that is taller (like a mini-van) to allow users more head-room clearance when loading and unloading coffins.

I got the chance to drive some of these cars when I worked at my rail yard job the years before getting the cemetery gig. They're big and intimidating and a little unsettling when you realize what they're used for. The cars are decorated like wedding dress shops to hide what's inside and the wagon area is lined with stainless steel so they can be hosed down and cleaned of any human fluids which are an unpleasant reality of burials.

The security guards were also asked on occasion to help move caskets in or out of the vehicles after staff went to pick them up from other locations or needed to deliver them to other cemeteries. I thought I'd had my fill as pallbearer at dozens of family funerals, but I got to do it even more frequently than should be normal in one's working day. We were brought in when the coffins were excessively heavy and there was minimal funeral staff on site.

Two caskets in particular were memorable as they were both made of steel, not oak or pine wood as is traditional in the funeral biz. It has become a new selling point as the steel is tempered and polished to look like a car paint job in brushed or candle-apple coatings. The first casket was sparkling metallic blue and featured airbrushed logos of the deceased man's favourite hockey team, The Toronto Maple Leafs, on the sides, and his name painted in two foot letters from head to foot on the lid. I was told the casket cost upwards of $20,000.

The second casket was a custom job as well for a bike gang member that had passed and his polished black steel casket was covered with flames and the iconic *Easy Rider* photo of Dennis Hopper and Peter Fonda airbrushed on the lid. The estimated cost was around $35,000. It had been paid for by a chapter of the Para-dice Riders.

I actually patrolled the day of his funeral and got to witness the hundreds of motorcycle *enthusiasts* that gathered to pay respects to one of their fallen brothers. A truly nicer bunch of guys I've never met. They lined their bikes up along the roadway leading to the gravesite and raised thermoses and Tim Hortons coffee cups filled with various refreshments in salute as the hearse rolled by. About a dozen guys stuck around after the ceremony to have an impromptu wake and invited me over for some coffee.

I'm not a coffee drinker, but I took the offering anyway. It was heartfelt gesture and these guys needed someone to talk to about their buddy. He'd suffered a heart attack and died on the road with his bike. As far as they were concerned it was a heroic way to go out because he was doing the thing he loved the most. I asked them where the motorcycle ended up and they said a lot of it had been melted down and used to create the casket. Life doesn't get more full-circle than that.

WHAT LURKS IN THE BASEMENT

Below the hearse garage was the basement where the cemetery kept all manner of decorations, chairs, tables, discarded headstones, and documents dating back to the 1800s. I never had reason to go down there unless I noticed a light on when locking up. The mission then was to determine if someone was still in the basement, secure the space, and turn the light off.

The basement was the length of the entire Visitation Centre and had a noisy furnace and rattling elevator in it.

The building was fairly new so it didn't have a particularly creepy vibe, but I was always on edge when I saw a light on down there. Did someone turn it on earlier or did it just come on by itself?

Your mind plays all kinds of tricks when you're alone. We were vigilant in always knowing how many staff members were on site at any given time. Was this someone I wasn't aware of? Did someone break in to steal a wreath like Nona liked to do? The very idea of a break-in was almost ludicrous, as it would mean getting through two keypad-secured doors from inside the private section of the building that was otherwise inaccessible to the public. Still, we took no chances. It could just as easily have been a disgruntled employee, though very unlikely.

On quiet nights, I'd actually go down to where the death records were kept and flip through the ancient ledgers full of names of the deceased looking for any sign that my family had been interred there before modern times. I never found a trace, but as an old records manager who had taken care of official documents for the City of Scarborough's Central Records in a previous life, it was fascinating to look at all that history in one place.

More interesting, however, were the old site photographs dating back to the earliest days of photography and the city itself. Many of the best pictures graced the walls of the buildings all over Beacon Hill, but the ones stored in the basement were still of great interest. They were usually shots of old graves and the landscape designs from days gone by. It was here that I found a shot of the old lake and the train that ran through the cemetery during its earliest incarnation. They were simpler, less secured, times.

A TISKET, A CASKET

One of the many rooms in the Visitation Centre that I had to secure and lock at the end of each night's patrol was the casket room. It's a lot like walking into a high-end furniture store for excessively rich people who have no sense of style. Or, if you prefer, a Sears department store to buy blinds or carpet. What you could buy there was a few dozen varieties of tombstones and caskets.

The funeral staff do their best to comfort families and not make the transaction sound like a pressure sale, but there's no way of couching the reality that they are there to close the deal and get the arrangements underway for the funeral itself. That meant picking out a head or foot stone and a coffin for their loved one as a representation of taste and luxury for all eternity.

The idea is superfluous when you understand that a good percentage of these caskets will end up in a cremation chamber. And, yes, the caskets do get put into the furnace despite what urban mythology has sprung up about unscrupulous funeral homes. Some places will rent caskets for bargain basement funerals, but that wasn't the case at Beacon Hill.

Otherwise, the caskets are buried and months later a head or foot stone, engraved as requested, is placed on the plot.

Imagine my surprise one evening during closing when I did a walkthrough of the casket room and found a young Filipino lady laying down in one of the demonstration caskets. She was part of the cleaning staff contracted to vacuum, mop, dust, and haul out the garbage from the offices and banquet rooms each night.

"Um…hello?" I said.

She began crawling out of the box and said, "I am sorry. I was just closing my eyes. We take turns sleeping because we work all night long."

"Don't sleep in the coffins, ma'am."

"I know. I know. Do not be mad."

"I'm not mad, but you're lucky I didn't lock you in here. I was about to shut off the light and lock the doors."

She gathered up her duster and spray bottles, and squeezed past me, "Have a good night."

This was one of many indiscretions we discovered about this particular cleaning crew. They didn't last long and were fired a few months after being hired mainly for doing a crappy job and I assume, for doing things like taking naps in the caskets.

CARPET CLEANERS

My one delight in working at Beacon Hill was when the carpet cleaners were on site. These guys would arrive late – usually close to when I needed to secure and lock the buildings – and stay all night cleaning the carpets. They had a van with a machine in it that pumped the water and fed the hoses used to wet-vac the mausoleums and the Visitation Centre. They only worked when there were no visitations at the cemetery.

I loved it when they were there because I only had to visually check the building at that point because they were responsible for locking down and setting the alarms long after I got to go home. It made for an easy final patrol of the site on those nights.

Of course, I had a rather sinister streak in me and would often double back and sneak into the building they were working in to scare the crap out of them. To drown out the noise of the machines, the two guys would listen to music through headphones and would never hear me approach. I would simply walk up to either one of them from behind and reach over their shoulder just enough so they could see my hand. The funeral directors often wore white linen gloves and I'd put one on to enhance the spook factor. It never failed to elicit a loud, blood curdling, scream out of both of them. We'd laugh and laugh.

OTHER WORKERS

Beacon Hill might very well be the largest recipient of fresh flowers I can think of. Thousands upon thousands of flowers annually. I'm not a big fan of growing flowers, cutting them down, and then shipping them off to people where they die within hours. It's a waste of the flowers and a huge, pointless, monetary expense. But I'm not their audience. The floral industry is big business and, as such, I was tasked with guiding drivers to the Visitation Centre or gravesides in the event of a last minute delivery.

The responsibility was a pain in the ass because I was also responsible for noting when the flowers arrived. People would pay for delivery based on a time sensitive arrangement. The flowers were to arrive before the funeral, not after it. I had to make note of who delivered what and when if there was no one on hand at the Visitation Centre to receive the delivery.

Sundays were usually one of those days as ceremonies weren't as frequent, and delivery trucks would show up late Sunday nights to beat the Monday morning delivery deadlines. Or they'd arrive a day late having missed a ceremony the day before. Many occasions were examples of the latter and the florists would have to refund grieving family members for a botched delivery.

More times than not they'd shotgun to the Visitation Centre, toss the flowers onto a workbench in the hearse garage, and leave undetected. I had to stop at the garage every hour to ensure that flowers hadn't 'magically' appeared.

Another frequent guest at the cemetery was Jimmy the Engraver. His job was exactly as described. He was responsible for engraving new epitaphs on gravestones that were already in place all over the cemetery. A new gravestone was pre-engraved and installed as part of the full funeral service offered by Beacon Hill. It was Jimmy's job to work on adding additional script to the same stone at a later date when other family members passed.

It was a hard, labour intensive job, and I was told that there are less than 15 guys in all of Canada still skilled enough to do the work in the field, as it were. It's one thing to engrave granite or marble while it's lying horizontal and flat on a work bench with precision machine shop tools, it's entirely another to work on a tombstone that's upright and vertical during sun, rain or snow.

Jimmy spent his time travelling every day to different graveyards all across the city. He'd come out twice a week to Beacon Hill because the workload was excessive. Sometimes he'd be there from when I opened at 7AM until the sun went down. He was limited by season as well because his mobile compressor and its water gun didn't work well in the freezing temperatures and so he didn't bother. He'd work his ass off for the 7 or 8 months of okay weather to build up his bank account and then take the winter off. It was hard to explain to families why sister

Mary June's name wasn't yet on the family grave marker despite it being −32C outside.

On those long hot days I'd see Jimmy on his knees in front of a slab of granite wearing a hood over his head to keep the dust from flying into his face and plying his craft. He could match the lettering style on a gravestone with precision – even old Gothic English script. I'd bring him coffee or water and often let him leave his trailer and compressor overnight in the utility yard if he needed to return the next day. It allowed him to squeeze in a few more jobs the next day because he didn't have to go back to his shop to load the gear. He was very appreciative. I was in awe of this dying art form and Jimmy himself - a true artisan.

CHAPTER EIGHT

ANIMALS (THREE DIFFERENT ONES)

Though dogs were a constant sight in the cemetery being led by owners with various levels of care and responsibility, they were a mostly controlled substance in my daily routine. The cats, deer, coy-wolves, and racoons, as thoroughly discussed in *True Tales From a Cemetery Cop*, were an unpredictable quantity and made for hours of entertainment. There were, however, a few other animal visitors that should be added to the Dr. Doolittle menagerie as well.

HAVE YOU SEEN THE MASSIVE PIGGY?

A nearby shopping plaza – where the bulk of the errant shopping carts seemed to derive – brought in a petting zoo to entertain kids during the summer months. The morning they brought the animals to the site the shipping trucks were lined up along a road between Section 2 and 3 and stood until the animals could be unloaded. There were donkeys, chickens, goats, geese, turkeys, rabbits and pigs.

My timing always seemed to be impeccable and on this day it was uncanny. As I pulled up to the gates to drive from Section 3 back across the street to Section 2, I was blocked by a pig. It was the size of a sofa and was determined to scoot around my car to get through the gate to the garden that was festooned with freshly planted flowers. The students unloading the truck were attempting to corral it back into the vehicle until they could get the other pigs moved safely down to the plaza. It wasn't going well. They had lost control of the porker.

The animal had no collar so there was nothing to grab onto. The students stood between the pig and my car waving their arms and yelling at it to turn around. It was a shake-my-head moment. I thought about helping them for about a split second but realized that this was way out of my league. I had my hand on the radio to call dispatch in case we needed to call animal control or 911 should the animal rampage.

After a lot of pulling and pushing and cajoling, someone waved a fistful of carrots at the beast and it turned. They led it by the nose back to the vehicle and it stood on the ramp defiantly demanding the fresh food. I pulled the car out of the gateway and went to lunch. The pig had made me hungry.

HAWK EYES

One of the various alternatives people can choose for a memorial ceremony at the cemetery is to release doves rather than the non-eco-friendly helium balloons favoured in the past. The doves come via a company that has trained handlers. The birds fly on command and return shortly after being set free to fly around the grounds.

The cemetery also had pair-bonded hunting red-tailed hawks that lived in the trees near the Visitation Centre. It was no mystery why. The doves became lunch on one occasion much to the general horror of the group of mourners on hand for the memorial presentation. To add insult to injury, the company supplying the birds would invoice the family for the loss of the bird(s). I'm not sure that anyone would have let that stand as it was an act of nature and the hawks didn't know any better. Circle of life, yada, yada.

I had my own encounter with the hawks one day when driving near the Visitation Centre when a rabbit ricocheted off the hood of my car only to be reclaimed within a split second by one of the red-tailed hawks. The hawk had clearly lost its grip on the animal and recovered without missing a beat. I spent the next hour in the hearse garage washing the blood and fur off the front of the patrol car.

OPOSSUMS AND SKUNKS

The grind of driving through the cemetery on unlit roads at night with nothing but a floodlight on the roof becomes routine and monotonous especially at the end of a 15-hour shift. You tune out the reflective surfaces on the polished gravestones and try and keep focused on the narrow winding turns in front of you. Imagine driving on a dirt road in the country on a moonless night. You've got limited visibility of less than a few hundred feet and the tree tops are so full of leaves it creates a dark canopy that makes the entire trek feel like you're passing through a forested tunnel.

The racoons usually kept away from any speeding vehicles and would scurry up trees or behind them for safety. Animals that don't fear the motion of bright lights in the dark are opossums and skunks. Both will stand where they are and put up a defiant stand.

Skunks I'd encountered at Beacon Hill in the daytime, which not unlike the daylight racoons, was unusual. The only one I came across at night decided to lead me down the road. I followed far enough behind it to not scare it into spraying the car. It eventually side-stepped me and headed into a glade.

The opossum, however, was not conceding any part of the roadway to me at all. I was taken aback as I'd never seen one in the wild before and certainly not one deep in the city. It sat and stared into the headlights of the patrol car. I redirected the floodlight on the roof hoping the 500W blinding light would annoy it enough to give it a nudge.

I was on a curve that had reinforced curbs on either side so driving around it was impossible without tearing out the bottom of the car or the grass or both. I had two choices. I could attempt to drive over it and hope I cleared the beat without it freaking out and running under the passing wheels like a mentally challenged squirrel or I could back up and turn around.

I backed up and turned around. I never saw it again and few people believed me when I mentioned the incident. There's a good chance it was someone's escaped pet and that it still lives in the cemetery.

A CAT UNLEASHED

All the cats at the cemetery were feral or house cats just out for leisurely strolls. The ones at the outdoor mausoleum that was in a perpetual state of repair never wandered much farther than the red cherry picker used by the construction crews. Occasionally, they'd wander out and hug the retaining walls near the gates, but never ventured inside the cemetery proper to the graves themselves.

This was significant to understand because a teenager often came to the cemetery with his pet cat sitting on one shoulder. The cat was a large black and white tuxedo, and was not only tame, but friendly to strangers as well. I'd often stop and pet the cat as I talked to the kid about the fact that the animal wasn't on a leash. Technically, he was able to skirt the rules because the bylaw only required dogs to be on leashes. I'd let him go and he'd be on his way.

One day I saw the two of them approach the Gothic mausoleum and the cat jumped down halfway up the stairs to the propped-open front doors. It was the only time I ever saw the cat climb down. The teen went inside and used the bathroom while the cat sat patiently waiting. When he came back out, the cat jumped back up as before. The cat was very well trained.

"Do you tell the cat to get down so you can go inside

to use the facilities?"

"No. She won't go inside. I don't think she likes the smell of dead things."

I thought about it and remembered seeing one stray cat run across the front steps, but never went inside. In fact, the racoons never crossed the threshold of the mausoleum either and the front doors were perpetually open from sun-up to sundown.

Only birds ever entered the mausoleum and would occasionally build nests in the rafters above the chapel. Their sense of smell was clearly used to the stench of death.

CREMATORIUM

The four-legged animals know enough to avoid death. The scent means imminent danger. We humans are drawn to it. Not the smell necessarily, but the need to cover it up and bury it like a dog. The other way of eliminating it, of course, is to burn the death away. From Viking warrior funeral pyres to mass cremations following deadly disasters, man has attempted to obliterate his own remains and return to the elements as ash. For it is written.

The Beacon Hill crematorium was a means to that end. Alonso was the chief undertaker there and he spent all day both comforting grieving families and getting them to trust that he would cremate their loved ones with grace and dignity. It was a tall order.

He walked me through the process one day. I wasn't prepared for it. It's a very methodical, mechanical, and entirely pragmatic operation in and of itself. All I saw was a body being sent to its final end. I couldn't separate the person from the corpse. To do his job properly, Alonso had to separate the two things. He was able to help the family emotionally, but he also needed to make sure that nothing went wrong in completing the task. I imagine it was the same type of role a minister might have to play when administering last rights before committing someone to the grave. There was definitely duty of care in both.

In the old days the crematorium required stoking a coal fire in a brick-walled retort (or cremation chamber). Beacon Hill had decommissioned its previous one after it was costing too much money to maintain. The modern version that Alonso ran had been built at the cost of millions of dollars and designed to emit the least amount of airborne pollutants of any cremation furnace in the country. The neighbourhood was beside itself over the installation of the new machine. Truth was that it put less pollution into the air than the tens of thousands of cars driving by the cemetery every day. Concerned citizens were not convinced.

This device took up most of the mausoleum's basement and was run by a state-of-the-art computer system. Alonso trained at the best schools in North America to learn how it operated. The furnace needed to be heated between 1400 and 1800 Fahrenheit to effectively break down the composition of a body. The temperature was determined by the combined body and casket weight and could be calculated to evaporate a body to within minutes.

The cremation would have to be witnessed by a family member or legal representative by law. Sometimes a family wanted a few people on hand. Their delay in arriving would mean Alonso was delayed in completing the cremation. On a productive day, Alonso could complete three cremations. Under pressure he could do four. The furnace ran seven days a week. Letting it cool off at any point meant waiting for it to heat up from dead cold which would take up to four hours. That was time the cemetery didn't have given the number of cremations it needed to do every single week. The service was highly in demand given the shift from ground burials to the more practical, and let's face it, cheaper cremations.

The entire process is unnerving. The machine is loud and ungodly. There is a viewfinder behind the furnace like you'd find on a telescope so that witnesses you can view the immolation. Alonso told me I could. I couldn't do it. Such a private and sacred event shouldn't be on display for strangers to ogle. I wouldn't want my own demise put on display – even in the secure environment of the crematorium. Alonso respected that, but then asked me to help him clean out the filter to collect the ashes of this particular individual.

This happened after I'd had the incident with the woman at the Visitation Centre that inhaled the ashes from a dropped urn, which I've discussed previously. I was only slightly less squeamish and nauseated this time. The most commonly asked question is whether families actually get the ashes from *their* loved ones following cremation. The answer is yes. The contents of the retort have to be cleared after each burn because the remnants of the casket – metal handles, nails, hinges – must be removed so as to not clog the furnace's intake and outtake filtering system.

We had breathing masks on as he pulled the filter out of a long tube with a pair of needle nose pliers. The filter was cracked and it would have to be changed. He poured the ashes into an ornate gold engraved urn as supplied by the deceased's family. He dusted the ash off of each piece of the casket into the vase as well. The brass handles and hinges were disposed of and he sealed the urn in a plastic bag and then the bag was placed in a non-descript cardboard box. He thanked me and said he needed to refit a new filter and so I left. I went to the bathroom and threw cold water on my face and scrubbed my hands for ten minutes. Crematorium undertaker is the second worst job imaginable.

THE WORST JOB IMAGINABLE

Funeral directors and assistants have the worst job. Don't believe me? Just ask them. They'll tell you so. On nights when there were no services at the Visitation Centre, I'd hang out with the staff as they wound down to the end of their shifts. Many times there was nothing but paperwork to push around and so the stories would start. It was a way to blow off steam and I was the newbie, relatively speaking, so they liked to see someone new squirm to their tales of blood and gore.

As I said at the beginning of this book, horror doesn't frighten me unless it's the psychological horror of cruel and humane people. The funeral staff came close to changing my mind.

Not all the staff was certified to handle the bodies. Many were trained in the hospitality trade to deal with people and organize the events at the Visitation Centre. The oldest director, Stanley, had been working at the cemetery for 13 years and was an undertaker and embalmer who had started at a private funeral home and eventually worked his way up the chain of command at Beacon Hill.

He came to the funeral industry later in life and was on the verge of retirement right when I started working at Beacon Hill. He'd seen enough. He wanted to sail into his sunset years doing happier things. He loved his job, but he wore every agonizing minute of everyone's collective grief on his face.

He was the one they called to dress corpses that had been in car accidents, wars, and in one case, a bear mauling. A husband and wife had gone camping in Northern Ontario to a small island and had been attacked by a bear in their sleep. He described how he was required to dress this woman who had been half eaten and then the husband who was missing an arm and had a hole in his chest that was shaped like the bear's paw.

Stanley had taken two years of training to learn how to apply makeup for all the unfortunate people who were expected to go on display during open casket ceremonies. He thought it was the cruellest end to a life well lived by being dressed like some mannequin in a wax museum. Against management's wishes he frequently talked families out of having open casket viewings. His would still work with the deceased to make them presentable, but only so the family could view the body later in private before the interment.

Despite it all, Stanley had a great sense of humour and it wasn't dark humour either. Come to think of it, all the funeral directors and assistants were unlike their environments. They came in cheerful, and remained cheerful, as was appropriate through the various stages of family counselling and guidance leading up to the funeral day itself. Bless each and every one of them.

CHAPTER NINE

THE OTHER MAUSOLEUMS

The Gothic mausoleum gets the bulk of the interesting stories because of its age, its creep factor, and the traffic moving through it. The other mausoleums were far more nondescript and charming as monuments to religion, and those who wrapped their loved ones in the arms of God. As a non-believer it was fascinating to me, but I always felt a sense of calm in contrast to the Gothic mausoleum which was always filled with gloom on top of the sorrow.

One of the smaller mausoleums was more like a general store as it was framed completely in glass. It was a single floor with a few couches in the foyer that divided two sectioned areas full of crypts. You could walk around the entirety of one end while the other end featured a fire exit. I could clear and secure the building in under two minutes.

On weekends the building attracted quite a few visitors. Around the perimeter were leather chairs and benches clearly donated from one of Canada's greener banking institutions, if you get my drift? The furniture was an audacious affront to all the balloons, cards, memorial candles and chotchkies people would leave in tribute to their family members.

There were two women who practically lived in the building. One was a very old Italian woman who barely spoke English. She was always impeccably dressed in black mourning wear and kept to herself. She would sit just inside the front door in one of the green chairs and read from scriptures. She only ever spoke to me once, and it was to tell me that a strange man had come into the mausoleum and was acting strange around her and the other woman.

The second woman was from the West Indies, much younger, and spoke English very well. She was also not quite in her right mind and spent most of her time at the mausoleum preventing people from entering the building. After seeing this strange man hanging around she doubled her efforts to barricade herself and the Italian lady inside. On this particular day, I had to talk her down off the ledge metaphorically speaking.

"Ma'am, you have to allow people to come see their loved ones just like you do."

"They're evil. They want to kill us."

"No one wants to kill you."

"That man tried to. He had that look in his eyes."

It was ironic considering the crazy eyes she was flashing at me.

"Ma'am. No one is trying to kill you."

"My brother was murdered, y'know. Don't talk to me about no one killing me."

"You could stay home where it's safe," I offered.

"My brother is here. I'm not leaving. They can leave. All of them. I paid $30,000 for my brother to be in here. I have the right to be here."

"Everyone else does as well."

The building could only be accessed by keying a number into a security keypad at the front door. Only the families of the interred knew the access number. The keypad would be smashed beyond use at least once a week. We suspected it was this West Indies woman smashing it with one of the rocks that could be found around mausoleum's garden so she and the old Italian woman would be locked in until it was time to leave. Everyone else would be locked out. There were a lot of complaints.

Management refused to do anything about her. The repair costs on the security system must have been huge, as there was a maintenance crew in every Monday trying to put it back together again. Their argument was that she did indeed pay for the privilege of having the door secure. It seemed she was getting anything but.

Securing the doors on the mausoleums was an eternal pain in the ass. The doors all had their quirks and the multi-story ones came with their own unique issue. When you design a building made of glass that is several floors tall, and have more than one exit door, the air pressure inside rises. On windy days that air pressure creates drafts and makes the doors difficult to keep airtight.

Keeping them airtight is necessary in setting the alarms. All the doors are rigged with magnetic strips that only operate when they are in parallel proximity to each other. If one door were pressed forward the air pressure would trigger a sensor that indicated that the door was open. It wasn't, but the security alarm control panel would read it as a breach. It became a maddening game of how-do-I-keep-the-fucking door-sealed night after night.

One of the mausoleums had a notoriously bad problem with this. The air pressure was so high in the building that if you didn't turn the deadbolt on the door it would blow open all by itself. But with the dead bolt engaged it would still bulge past the trigger point for setting the security alarm. The control panel believed the door was always open.

I frequently had to call another staff member to come and help me hold the door steady while I set the alarm. After a few times doing this the alarm would go off as the door would pop far enough out to trip the gap in the magnetic strip. Many times this would happen in the dead of night. The alarm company would call dispatch at some ungodly hour and a mobile unit would have to go to Beacon Hill and try to secure the mausoleum all over again. It's why *they* got paid the big bucks.

Management finally sent the alarm company execs in to move the magnetic strips once and for all. They solved that problem and another one cropped up. A different door in the building began to show that it was open as well.

During a shift change back at the security off one morning I mentioned to Billy how I was having this problem and he laughed.

"Why don't you just bypass the door alarm?"

"I would but I don't know how to do it on that old alarm keypad."

He wrote the procedure out on a scrap of paper and the next time it happened I just re-routed the alarm so it would ignore *any* door that wasn't co-operating.

BOOK OF REMEMBRENCE

One of the services that the cemetery offers is a ledger in each of the mausoleums marking the passing of those interred there by date of death. They are housed in glass cases and can be viewed each day as visitors enter the buildings. As security guards, we were required to open the cases and flip the book page to the next day as we locked up the mausoleums each night. If the page were blank, we'd advance the book until there was an entry. Sometimes there'd be no memorial inscriptions for a week, but failure to make sure the book was up to date was punishable by reprimand.

The issue, however, was access to the key for the showcases. Each was built with different locking mechanisms. One required a skeleton key, one an Allen key, and the others with regular keys found on any glass cases you'd see in jewellery stores. The Allen key was always on the cemetery key ring we would get from the lock box on the front gate of Beacon Hill when we entered the grounds each day. That key ring also had keys to the padlocks on the gates and the master key for the doors on site.

The other showcase keys were supposed to be hung on hooks in janitor rooms. Occasionally, they'd be missing and we'd have to call around looking for them. Many times they'd been left on desktops or had fallen on the floor. I never had a problem eventually finding what I needed and the books would have their pages advanced as needed.

THE CHAPEL ORGAN

I wish I played keyboards. I used to noodle on them when I was a musician. The most I could muster was the melody to "I Just Can't Get Enough" by Depeche Mode. Real playing was beyond my scope. More the shame then when I realized that the chapel in the Gothic mausoleum contained an authentic Hammond B3 with a Leslie speaker in it. Double the shame when the maintenance crew advised me one day that they'd trashed it and the speaker. I raced around back to find the entire rig in the dumpster – smashed and useable.

They explained that it had actually been sitting collecting dust for over a year. It was in need of so much repair work that it was cheaper to just have services performed on rented electric keyboards brought in from the Visitation Centre. It was to weep.

BLACK FLIES. THE LITTLE BLACK FLIES

The cemetery office building was originally the headquarters for the train master of the railway that once crossed the property. The tracks were long gone, but a section of the bridge they were built on was still attached to the office. It was refitted with cobble stones, and a bench, and made for a nice seating area to overlook the waterfall, fountain, and Memorial Atrium out back.

The office was well over 80 years old and on a sump pump system rather than city sewer services. It smelled its age and the staff frequently complained about tiny black flies all over the building. They were mostly concentrated near the basement hallway leading to and from the bathroom plus the stairwell leading up to the board rooms and reception area.

These weren't the same insects found in the mausoleums. Those bugs lived off the decay of dead bodies. These flies looked like moths shrunk to the size of Rice Crispies. They began to proliferate like the attic scene in *The Amityville Horror*. Emily, the receptionist, was beside herself trying to keep all the doors from the basement closed so the thousands of them wouldn't invade the boardrooms while the public was making funeral arrangements. She berated the cemetery manager to do something about it. He finally relented when he found the flies had gotten into the employee kitchen's fridge.

Pest control and a plumbing company finally arrived to try and get rid of the nasty little fliers. Both teams gave up after an hour or two saying they didn't think they could eliminate them. Pest control believed the larvae had been in the sump overflow tank for more than a decade and wasn't sure what finally brought them to life. Their best guess was that there could be over a million flies trying to hatch.

It's interesting to note that the sump is located under

a section of the old train bridge that had collapsed and killed two people in 1929. *Amityville*, indeed.

BEES IN THE BONNET

The staff building in Section 3 was once an old private school. It's three stories tall and is frequently used to hold training sessions for Beacon Hill's staff and for the arborists to have a place to plan their annual tree inventory in the cemetery. The building's upper floors contain rooms that were bedrooms at one time and the whole place has crooked floors and in need of restoration and/or a tear down.

Visitors to the cemetery frequently complained about bees near the building. Pest control determined that there was a nest under a public washroom next to the building. They spent two days relocating the hive. Several days later staff noticed that the bees were still flying around the staff building.

A bee specialist was brought in from another city and he realized the bees had built a hive on the drain pipe where it met the eaves trough and the downspout. He asked me if he could go up to the room in the far corner where the hive was so he might be able to get access to it through an upper window.

I let him in and we went into the building and up the stairs, but I didn't have a key to the specific room he needed. I called the assistant site supervisor, Mark, and asked him to bring the key. He arrived a few minutes later and the three of us pushed into the room.

Much to our shock and horror, the wall in the corner of the room nearest the outside drain pipe was missing all its ancient horse-hair plaster from ceiling to floor. The planks were exposed and we could see thousands of bees coming into the room from outside. The room was a cacophony of buzzing. The bee expert had entered the room ahead of us. He turned and told Mark and I to leave. We did as he asked and he closed the door behind us.

We headed down to street level and saw the man hanging out of one of the upstairs window.

"We're going to need to bring a conservation crew in here. I can't tell yet, but I think there's two hives. That means two Queens. I want to relocate them to my Conservatory in Niagara."

Mark seemed put out, "Okay. I'll let management know. We'll have to close the building to foot traffic, I guess."

We waited for the bee wrangler to come back down; I secured the rest of the building and set the alarm. The relocation process took nearly a week, but I was happy to see that they managed to get every bee off site without any known casualties.

CHAPTER TEN

CLEAR AND PRESENT DANGER

In the grand scheme of things I, like most of the visitors at Beacon Hill, have had mostly innocuous experiences there. My frequency and duration of work hours at the cemetery enhanced the number of unusual and alarming incidents but I consider myself lucky to have missed some of the more dangerous days on the job.

Following the release of *True Tales From a Cemetery Cop* I revisited my old stomping ground and talked to a number of different guards and staff I was still in contact with. They volunteered some of the more extraordinary stories that have grown into cemetery folklore now. There was almost a nostalgic whimsy in the recounting of what were seriously bad situations. It's a strange dichotomy to wish for a time when the world was less safe, but the events were more exciting. One guard put it best when he said, "At least we earned our keep back then. Now we bust dog walkers, drink coffee, and write reports all day while we watch our stomachs and asses grow fatter."

POLICE AND THIEVES

There are a lot of banks near Beacon Hill. So many, in fact, that robbing them used to be a sporting affair, and hiding in the cemetery was the quickest means of throwing the police off the trail.

Alonso told me about the time that he and another employee were going about their business preparing the crematorium for a cremation one morning when a S.W.A.T. team busted through the loading dock doors. A phalanx of cops pushed them both to the floor, face down, with their hands behind their heads. There was a lot of screaming and pointing at the duo with automatic weapons.

Apparently, two people had robbed a nearby bank and were spotted entering the cemetery. They had shot a bank teller so the Metro Police were on high alert and wound up tight like a spring. Alonso and his assistant both produced their employee badges and I.D.'s and the police released them. The cops were concerned that the robbers would disguise themselves as employees to evade detection. They were right.

While more cops rolled into the cemetery and blocked the exits several of the summer students had been robbed at gunpoint of their work clothes which included T-shirts with Beacon Hill logos. The robbers kept to the fence line by one of the mausoleums, but were spotted as they tried to climb over a fence by another cemetery employee. By this point, the grounds were being evacuated and the employee radioed in to the security guard on duty. The guard was Billy who passed the info onto police services who, in turn, zeroed in on the location of the robbers within seconds.

A second S.W.A.T. team moved in as the culprits attempted to access a backyard not far from the old cemetery house where I'd evicted some picnicking women years later. One robber was tazered and the other surrounded and taken down without any shots being fired.

BILLY DON'T BE A HERO

There is an underbelly to living in the big city and it's a sad fact that crime looms large in nearly every neighbourhood. Though the underclass had been mostly pushed out of the Beacon Hill neighbourhood, the cemetery was an equal opportunity burial ground. If you have the money you can rest there for all eternity. Crime lords and gang members are no exception.

Billy had no tolerance for gang-bangers. These were suburban kids with nothing to lose except a reputation and most often their lives. Because Billy had gone to war he saw street violence as nothing but children trying to imitate adults on the battle field. In either example people were going to get killed.

The number of interments for the victims of gang violence was mounting and the Metro police took every opportunity to embed undercover cops in the cemetery to tail people visiting the graves of gang-bangers or the funerals of same.

For obvious reasons they never identified themselves very often to cemetery staff or security guards though I did manage to befriend one briefly when he showed up every night right around closing time wanting to sit inside the gates while I closed up.

If I knew there was going to be a gang funeral, which was obvious to anybody paying attention, I kept a distance in the patrol car and had my finger on 911 speed-dial. Billy, on the other hand, attempted to keep the peace with the gang members. He always feared that rival gangs might crash the interment ceremonies and he'd need to call back-up and/or protection for himself and the mourners. Having been in Desert Storm he believed he was prepared for any situation. One time he let his guard down (no pun intended).

Two brothers had been killed in a drive-by shooting and the funeral became pretty high profile. Hundreds of people showed up from the boys' neighbourhood, relatives, and presumably rival gang members *and* undercover cops.

Billy attempted the standard traffic control procedures in his patrol car as the section where the interments were proceeding was pretty narrow for car access and needed to be kept clear. He rolled his window down and made a snide comment about some rather tough looking gang-bangers that had parked their cars on the grass. These individuals didn't take kindly to being told what to do and they stepped in front of the patrol car to block his access. He stuck his head out the window and told them to get off the road. They surrounded the car. There were six of them.

One came to the driver's window and pulled back his long coat to reveal a gun, "You gonna tell a n*gga what to do, you old white fuck?"

The group laughed. If Billy was scared he didn't flinch.

"You must be deaf. I said get off the fucking road. Or are you too stupid to know that the police would drop you where you stand in a heartbeat? They're watching us talk right now."

Billy was bluffing. He hoped that the undercover cops were watching. He had no way of knowing for sure.

The kid backed off and waved the others away but never broke eye contact. Billy drove past the burial ceremony and sniped from the other side of the congregation in his car. When the ceremony was over the mourners cleared out without incident and Billy went about patrolling the rest of the cemetery. Soon he noticed a car following him. He assumed it was one of the undercover cops coming to debrief him on the conversation Billy had with the gang-bangers.

Billy pulled to the side and waited for the other car to pull up so they could communicate through the drivers' windows. Except it was the same gang-bangers, and the one in the passenger seat had a gun pointed at his head through the window.

"Well if it isn't the old white fuck! Try mouthing off to us now, bitch."

According to Billy, he managed to talk his way out of getting shot. Now it was sundown and these tough thugs were starting to get nervous about being in the cemetery after dark. There's nothing more pathetic than being a criminal who is superstitious about the Bogeyman.

Billy offered to lead them out of the cemetery if they'd just relax. It's exactly what he did. As they got to the entrance gate he pulled over and ushered them through. As he got out to close the gates behind them, a battalion of police vehicles stormed the intersection and arrested them.

Billy found out later that two of the six guys in the car had warrants for their arrest on weapons infractions and other crimes. One was possibly connected to the murder of the two brothers who'd been buried that day. The police waited to arrest them off private property so as to not involve the cemetery. Billy was pissed that he'd nearly been killed and that no one had told him the plans. He would have escorted them off site a whole lot earlier than he did.

SEASONAL EMPLOYEE FROM HELL

Every spring Beacon Hill has an open call for seasonal employees to help with ground maintenance from April through September. These are the people who work tirelessly mowing grass, clearing leaves, planting flowers, and generally keeping the site immaculately groomed. It is their diligence that has given Beacon Hill its reputation as the parkland that isn't a public park. If there weren't people buried there it could easily be a campground.

A recurring seasonal employee at the cemetery was in a small traffic altercation with a Buddhist priest up the street from the cemetery. The priest was a regular who did religious services at the cemetery. The two were familiar with each other. However, the employee was driving a company vehicle at the time of the accident having gone to get coffee at a local donut shop during a break and didn't want to report the accident to his bosses or the Beacon Hill administrators. The cemetery truck was no worse for wear, but the Buddhist's car needed several thousand dollars in repairs. The seasonal employee said he'd pay the damage and begged the Buddhist not to report the incident to his own insurance company.

However, that night the seasonal employee got a call from the Buddhist saying he wanted to report the accident to his insurer. He needed the car for work and couldn't wait until the seasonal employee, who was barely clearing minimum wage, was going to make good on his promise to cover the costs. The employee said he'd come around the next day with half the money if he promised not to report the incident. He was afraid of losing his job if the incident was investigated.

The next day the employee took another company truck out to complete the errand during his morning coffee break as the Buddhist lived nearby.

The employee returned from the meeting with a bandaged arm and sat down in the lunch room with other staff to eat a hearty breakfast. The staff asked him what had happened and he said he'd mangled it while operating a hedge trimmer on site. He was encouraged to file a health and safety report, but he insisted to all of them that it was nothing and that he'd been careless and not paying attention.

Everyone went about their day without much concern until shortly before the end of the workday when several police cruisers cordoned off the cemetery and arrested the seasonal employee.

As the media reported during the trial, a meeting did take place at the Buddhist's home. They argued about the money as the employee didn't actually have any to give and the ongoing threat of reporting the incident to the insurance company. In a fit of rage, the employee stabbed the priest who later died in hospital.

As it turned out the priest had written everything down and his adult son knew that the meeting was to take place. So when police arrived at the crime scene, they knew immediately where to find the assailant.

During the trial, the employee said he'd acted out of self-defence, but forensics showed that the priest had been stabbed 31 times and his chest had been crushed. By all indications the employee had been sitting on his chest at the time of the stabbing. He was sentenced to life in prison.

The Buddhist's family did not hold the cemetery responsible and allowed the priest to be buried on the site as it was a place he enjoyed giving services when he was alive. He rests in a small plot behind the Gothic mausoleum's utility building where the seasonal employee had once worked.

This is the same utility building where every night the lights in the lunchroom come on long after security secures and locks the building down. The staff believes that it's the ghost of the Buddhist priest.

SUICIDE SQUAD

Beacon Hill Cemetery has a large interment of war dead. From the gothic nature of the place you'd expect most to be from the First or Second World Wars, but there are interments of more modern conflicts on site as well. Several Canadian soldiers from the Afghanistan conflicts are interred there.

Unknown to many of us is the fact that the Canadian military, specifically the Defence Department, takes care of its own. Unless requested by family to be a public ceremony, many soldiers killed in action or war vets who have succumbed after the fact, have very private services. The hows and whys of interment are kept strictly confidential with the cemetery's administrative staff. Even the gravediggers don't know the identity of the deceased – which is not standard protocol with other people buried there – until after the memorial stone or grave marker is installed many months later.

What should have been an average shift by one guard turned into a personal nightmare for him and many of the cemetery staff when he attempted to open the cemetery one morning and was met by members of the Canadian Army's elite police force. They wouldn't let him open the cemetery as usual. Within minutes the cemetery ground staff had begun arriving and they were also prevented from entering the site.

The cemetery manager soon arrived and the staff was allowed into one section but had to go directly to their offices and utility buildings. They were told not to leave the buildings until notified. The security guard and the cemetery manager were escorted to another section of the cemetery where they came upon many military vehicles, unmarked cars, and mechanical vehicles sporting large spotlights. These vehicles were surrounding a late model sedan that was covered with a tarp.

The security guard and cemetery manager were debriefed and questioned for nearly an hour. The security guard had been on shift the day before and they wanted to know if he'd seen the car in question anytime that day. To the best of his recollection he hadn't.

The intensity of questions increased and the guard was grilled harder about why he'd failed to see the vehicle. The protocol for security is that all vehicles must be accounted for and/or towed off site before he/she can leave the cemetery grounds each and every night. These protocols were implemented for two reasons: sexual assault or suicide.

This was the latter.

The deceased man in the car was an Afghanistan War vet who survived a particularly bad ambush with his squad. One of his compatriots did not survive and was returned home to be buried at Beacon Hill. The surviving soldier was suffering severely with PTSD and his family feared he'd harm himself having attempted to do so on several occasions previously. It was the anniversary of the other soldier's death and this officer was taking it particularly hard. He hadn't told anyone where he was going, but his family called the military to check the cemetery because they feared the worst.

The elite police force had arrived in the middle of the night and entered the cemetery by their own means. The soldier would have been in the cemetery with his vehicle before the gates were closed by the security guard at 10PM the night before. The insinuation was that the soldier might still be alive had the guard done his job properly and inspected every one of the back roads as per standard protocol. It looked like the guard did not do a final drive through before locking the main gates and signing-off his shift the night before. However, the guard's defence was that the patrol car didn't have a spotlight and with the cemetery being pitch black, a dark sedan against the dark trees would have been nearly impossible to spot.

The upshot of the incident is that the guard either quit (from grief) or was fired. Logic would dictate that spotlights be added to the cemetery patrol cars moving forward. Unfortunately, it would take a second life threatening case to change the way the security company and the cemetery handled extreme emergencies.

PREDATOR

In the summer following the military suicide, an elderly woman had gone to visit her husband's grave as a matter of routine. She had entered the cemetery on foot and several hours later in the dark a security guard found her beaten and bleeding near the side of one of the roads in Section 1.

The guard was quick to call 911. Response time was immediate. EMS quickly ascertained that she'd been raped, beaten, and then raped some more near the grave of her husband. She was rushed away and spent a very long time in the hospital. It became a city-wide story and one that the cemetery had a hard time defending itself against. The woman's family sued the cemetery, the security company, and the guard who was on duty that night.

The guard was questioned by the police and the same story played out as before. Regular mobile patrols were hourly on the site, but without a spotlight on the vehicle the chances of catching any strange activity would have been a matter of dumb luck. The woman and her assailant were on foot. She'd been dragged far into the burial area where a patrol car was unlikely to help catch anyone even in the daylight. The cemetery was that big and hiding spots were unlimited.

The guard was placed on leave as the lawsuit from the family was launched. Fortunately, the rapist was caught and put on trial. He was found guilty and sent to jail for a long time. His testimony confirmed the guard's story. He had dragged the woman to a spot where no one would have seen them. The guard was absolved, but it took a heavy toll on him. He felt responsible for the attack as I think any of us in that job would have. The case took three years to clear the court and the guard had a heart attack while stressing over the outcome. When last I heard, he was on a disability pension and unable to return to duty.

The upshot of this incident was more stringent patrol and emergency response protocols, the installation of emergency telephones at every cemetery gate (except the ravine) and spotlights on the patrol cars. This is how the job was presented to me when I started my security gig at Beacon Hill and remains in place to this day. There have been no incidents of this nature since.

CHAPTER ELEVEN

WHEN I WAS HERE

During my year-long run at Beacon Hill, March 9th, 2015 became an auspicious occasion. It was my sixth month as *Verm Blart: Cemetery Cop* and it would have been the 99th birthday of my maternal grandmother Marjorie Barker. As hard as it is to believe, these two things are connected. Bear with me and I'll explain.

Grandma Barker passed on July 29, 2011 at the ripe old age of 95. Feisty right up until a stroke took her motor skills the previous autumn; she was a mainstay in my life and that of the whole bickering, battling, and jovial Barker clan. You'd swear we were Irish by the amount of infighting we do. However, we actually come from St. Giles, Northamptonshire in England and it was dear old William Charles Barker who brought the personal struggles from there to Seagrave, Ontario, Canada in 1905.

Grandma's feistiness was reactionary and was rooted elsewhere. She was born a Booth. A clan that originated with David Joseph Blanchard Booth from Yorkshire, England and an émigré to Canadian shores in 1890. Come to think of it, maybe being embattled is a British thing stemming from a time when abject poverty and industrial wealth defined and divided a nation. Not unlike the world we now find ourselves in.

Marjorie's parents were scrappy too. David's daughter, Gladys Booth, grew up in a family of boys at 19 Steiner Avenue in a rundown ghetto east of the Don River in the City of York (later Toronto). It was an era of town reserved mostly for several generations of Irish immigrants displaced by the endless famines through the mid-1800s.

Gladys was born in 1897 and married Robert Winter on June 18, 1913 at the age of 16. They lived with the Booths in the Steiner house to raise a child named Muriel who was born the same year. That would have made the child scandalously illegitimate. Sadly, poor Muriel passed in the summer of 1915 as did a second child two months later. By the end of the year, Gladys found herself pregnant a third time, but the Great War was raging overseas and the Canadian government came knocking at all the doors on Steiner Avenue looking for eligible men to fight the good fight.

Robert Winter enlisted in the Canadian Expeditiary Forces and reported for duty in September 1915. It would mean a better and steadier income which the military would mail back to Gladys, and there would be a small pension should Robert arrive back at home alive following the Great War.

Robert reported for duty with the 58th Battalion at Niagara-On-The-Lake. The troops embarked for Great Britain on November 22, 1915. The battalion disembarked to France on February 22, 1916 and fought as part of the 9th Infantry Brigade (3rd Canadian Division) in France and Flanders until the end of the war.

Robert's paycheque came in as it should to support Gladys and as a supplement to the Booth household. My grandmother Marjorie was born prematurely March 9, 1916 while Robert was stationed in France. Granny was kept in the woodstove as a makeshift incubator. She wasn't expected to live and as such her birth was never officially recorded with the City of York Registrar. Instead, it was placed on record in the family Bible under the watchful eye of God.

Robert, meanwhile, found himself in a shitload of trouble. His recently declassified military records show that he was in the hospital at least three times and court-martialled for insubordination on one occasion. One hospital stay was for scabies, another for gashing his forehead while walking under a fortified bridge. It's unknown whether he was on patrol, but he certainly never saw combat action in France. The court martial was for going AWOL and he was docked four month's salary – a fact that didn't go unnoticed back in Canada on Steiner Avenue. He was drunk, unlucky or trying to be Canada's answer to *M.A.S.H.*'s Corporal Klinger in hopes of vying for a Section 8. Regardless, Robert spent the final months of the war and a good portion of 1919 in the hospital.

When he returned to Canada in late summer that year, Little Marge was already three years old. Robert was a stranger to both her and his wife, Gladys. He was either an established drinker or it became a post-war proclivity and Gladys was having none of it. She couldn't rely on him as a provider even with him present and accounted for. She soon kicked his ass to the curb. Gladys rarely spoke of him again except to say that he was a "scoundrel". No one saw him again after the divorce in 1926 including my Grandma Marjorie.

My great granny suffered socially for this. A woman just didn't instigate a divorce in the 1920s. She and Marjorie became outcasts even among the Booth clan. But Gladys was already independent and had serious skills as a farm hand, a nanny, and a maid. They'd make due, even without the support of her family, and they did. By the mid-1920s she'd met another man, Richard Herbert Smithson, a no-nonsense farmer, and they got married in 1927 if not entirely for love than as a stable home for Marjorie. Herbert played reluctant, but dutiful, surrogate Dad.

Marjorie eventually married my Grandfather Barker, also named Herbert, and they had many kids – my ever cantankerous, but big-hearted aunts and uncles. The couple lost a child in 1946 in a brother to my Mom and her siblings. My grandma Marge never got over it.

I have to believe Herbert Barker never did either. I've

been told he never drank until after this tragedy. But like my great granny, Marge had to do battle with Granddad's demons. They parted ways long before I can remember. He would die at the age of 67 in 1982, not long after Gladys. Marge would outlive him by 28 years.

And here's where my personal life and my job converged.

My days and nights as a Cemetery Cop meant patrolling Beacon Hill's endless roads past the grave of a cousin I'd lost when I was 11 years old from childhood leukemia named Wendy Barker. Not far from there is my Dad's mother, Shierene Vernon, and my step-grandfather Larry Hains. Only a hundred feet away is Herbert Barker's grave who rests alongside one of his sisters. His other sister is with her husband very close to the Visitation Centre.

Deep in the heart of the cemetery is the unmarked grave of Gladys Booth Winter Smithson and her second husband Herbert Smithson. Long before I worked the cemeteries I had gone looking for her grave to add to my family tree on Ancestry.com. To my frustration I could not find a headstone. With the help of Beacon Hill's office staff (Emily didn't work there yet), I did find the grave's plot one day in the rain.

Farther to the east, against a fence is the Field of Lost Souls - the nickname given to a section of the cemetery where children are buried. It is here where my Mom's baby brother Bruce Barker, who passed in 1946, is interred. His grave is also unmarked. Grandma Marge Barker's last wish was to be buried with him. I hope one day we can have her ashes interred with him. I also hope we can put markers on Gladys and Marge's final resting spots. They both grew up in simpler, less ostentatious times and didn't believe in pomp and circumstance for the dead. But in the absence of stories like this one and a static entry on Ancestry.com, a gravestone might be the only evidence to which they can declare "when I was here" to the world.

And what of Robert Winter?

He remarried and had another daughter, but I have yet to find out their fates. After finding the grave of his father and sister (and her husband) at Beacon Hill, I finally tracked down Robert's grave based on the information provided in the declassified National Archive war documents. The "scoundrel" passed in 1978 and received a full military burial at York Cemetery in North York, Ontario, alongside other members of the C.E.F. 58th Battalion from World War I. I never knew him, but I'm glad I found him even if my family disowned him.

We all share the same fate and deserve to be remembered after we shuffle off this earth. It is left up to the living to come and plant flowers, and mow the grass, and lay wreaths at Christmas. If nothing else, the cemetery is a three dimensional family tree we need to cultivate and memorialize because without memories by those still living we are nothing but names in a database at the cemetery head office. That's an awful way to spend the rest of eternity.

I encourage others to write their stories. Find out who your family is before there's no one left to ask. I've been lucky to have family members who have lived extraordinarily long lives. Document their lives. Share it with your children or nieces and nephews. Pass the info along and pay tribute to them at graveside every now and then. It's good for the soul…theirs and yours.

ABOUT THE AUTHOR

Jaimie "Captain CanCon" Vernon has been president of Bullseye Records of Canada Inc. since 1985. He wrote, edited, and published *Great White Noise* magazine in the 1990s, has been a musician for 38 years, and recently discovered he's been happily married to Sharon for 20 years.

He is also the author of the two volume *Canadian Pop Music Encyclopedia*s, a collection of his most popular 'Don't Believe A Word I Say' columns called '*Life's A Canadian...BLOG*', a biography of his early musical career called '*Life's A Canadian...Punk: Who Wants Guns - The Swindled Story 1973 - 1983*', and most recently, '*True Tales From a Cemetery Cop*'.

Jaimie also has two adult children named Danielle and Riley, and most recently became a grandpa to the adorable April.

For more information about Jaimie or the Cemetery Cop books, appearances, book signings, etc. check out these contact points:
http://www.cemeterycop.com
https://www.facebook.com/Cemetery-Cop-148271768946872/
https://www.facebook.com/jaimievernon

Email: gwntertainment@gmail.com
Twitter: @cemeterycop

True Tales From A Cemetery Cop

Made in the USA
Columbia, SC
22 September 2017